# kids on toast

Food glorious food! Welcome to the "Kids on Toast"
Inside you will find a magical array of recipes, ideas and most
importantly inspiration. As children growing up you must all
remember something about the food you were fed. We did! Some
of the best bits must be licking the spoon with that yummy cake
mixture all over it! Food, children and our country and culture have
evolved at a fast pace since we were both kids. Now we have kids of
our own, times have changed somewhat. Nutrition plays probably
the biggest part in a child's development and diet is important.
Everything in moderation of course! Sometimes it can be difficult to
try and balance home life, work life and playtime.

Food doesn't need to be complicated; try to keep things seasonal and
plan ahead. It's a great education for the kids to learn about how
food grows and when it is at its best. Make them part of it and inspire
them. After all, let's be honest, they inspire us! Most of all enjoy
yourselves doing it! They are our future after all and the reason why
this fantastic recipe book has been put together.

The rest is now down to you. We seriously hope you enjoy the book,
in fact, we know you will.

Keep it fresh, keep it simple and keep this book to hand.

Long live glorious food!!

Chris & James

The Tanner brothers

# kids on toast - a cookbook by kids, for everyone!

This book is the culmination of months of hard work by the parents, children and teachers of Yealmpton Primary School in Devon. Children and parents chose some of their favourite family recipes, and the children drew the wonderful pictures in class. There is a huge variety of recipes to suit all tastes, many are quick and simple for healthy nutritious family meals, others are treats for special occasions. Since the school kitchen became independent two years ago from the local authority, our school chef Chris Collum has been trying out all sorts of new ideas for the children's lunches. This has helped stimulate the children's interest in healthy eating which coupled with their work in class has led to this book's creation.

The proceeds from the sales of Kids on Toast will go towards our schools grounds project which includes creating an outdoor classroom, restoring a pond and orchard, and getting the children more involved in growing their own seasonal produce in our school allotment.

**Yealmpton School**
**Cookbook Committee**

# a word on healthy eating for school age children...

You will enjoy trying out the huge variety of recipes included in this book.

For children to stay fit and well and to grow into healthy adults, a balanced diet including fruit, vegetables & starchy foods is essential, with occasional treats.

**Fruit and vegetables**
at least 5-a-day, to provide vitamins and iron

**Bread, potatoes & other cereals**
at least one food from this group at each meal to provide energy, B vitamins, fibre, iron & zinc

**Milk & dairy foods**
3 servings of milk, yoghurt or cheese every day for protein, calcium, iodine & B vitamins

**Lean meat, fish, eggs, pulses & nuts**
having foods from this group twice a day provides protein, vitamins and minerals and omega 3 fats

**Foods high in fat & sugar**
these are high in calories but poor in nutrients, and eating too many foods such as fizzy drinks, cakes, crisps and biscuits can lead to obesity which can cause diabetes & heart disease in later life

**Alison White – Paediatric Diabetes Specialist Nurse**
Sources: British Dietetic Association Paediatric Group

**www.eatwell.gov.uk**
**www.food.gov.uk**

# Contents

Simply starters

Marvellous mains

Perfect puds

Bon appetit!

Pack a picnic

Barmy baking

Celebrity chefs & talented teachers

# simply
# starters

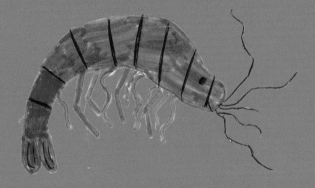

# reid's tomato soup

- **tinned tomatoes** ● **carrots** ● **celery**
- **onion** ● **stock cube** ● **425ml hot water**

Finely chop all ingredients. Fry onions for 2 – 3 minutes. Add celery and carrot to onions and fry for a further 2 minutes. Mix stock cube with 425ml hot water. Add mixed stock and chopped tomatoes to other vegetables, bring to the boil and simmer for 20 minutes. Liquidise, season to taste and serve.

Reid Jones

I love to eat homemade pizza.

# carrot soup

**● 50g english butter ● 350g carrots, peeled, diced or grated ● 2 leeks or onions, washed and sliced ● 450ml chicken stock ● salt and freshly ground pepper ● 150ml milk ● 6tbsp fresh single cream ● chopped fresh parsley to garnish**

Melt the butter in a large pan and fry the carrots and leeks/onions for 5-10 minutes. Add the stock and seasoning and simmer for a further 15-20 minutes. Sieve or puree the soup in a blender and return to the pan. Alternatively, cook vegetables for a further 10 minutes then beat with a wooden spoon. This adds texture to the soup. Stir in the milk and fresh cream, adjust seasoning and heat, but do not boil. Pour into a hot soup tureen and sprinkle with parsley.

Stephen & Naomi McMahon

Naomi: I like to eat noodles and apples. I help mummy make cakes and buns.

Stephen: I love to eat chips and I like carrots. At home I make cakes.

# creamy leek and potato soup

- **2 medium potatoes, peeled and cubed**
- **3 large leeks, washed and halved lengthways and sliced**
- **I medium onion, peeled and diced** ● **½ red pepper, chopped into small pieces** ● **2 vegetable stock cubes**
- **2 tsp dried herbs** ● **¼ tsp pepper** ● **¼ tsp curry powder**
- **¼ tsp chilli powder** ● **pinch of salt** ● **water to cover**
- **50 floz of cream** ● **drop of oil** ● **I clove of garlic**

Chop the vegetables. Heat oil and soften the onions. Add herbs and spices. Mix well then add the leeks, potatoes and pepper. Cover with water and add stock cubes. Bring to the boil then simmer for about 20-30 minutes until the potatoes are soft. Mash with a potato masher or use a hand blender to make into the consistency that you require. Add cream and salt and pepper to taste.

Tegan Thompson

I love pizza and strawberries. At home I help make tea.

# crab and sweetcorn soup

● **500g fresh mixed crab (white and brown crab meat)** ● **12 seafood sticks** ● **2 tins creamed sweetcorn**
● **1 egg**

Heat the creamed sweetcorn in a pan on a low heat. Finely chop the seafood sticks and add these with the crab to the pan of sweetcorn. Stir until boiling then remove from heat. Whisk the egg. Stir in the egg until mixture is white. Then serve.

Megan Welsh

I love burgers. I also like fruit salad. In the kitchen I help clean up.

# chicken liver pâté

● **1 onion** ● **1 clove garlic** ● **75g butter** ● **200g chicken livers** ● **fresh parsley and thyme (small handful)** ● **1 dessert spoon brandy**

Chop onion and garlic and soften in 25g of butter.

Add chicken livers and fry for 2-3 minutes, add

chopped herbs and rest of butter.  Then add brandy,

put into food processor and process until smooth.

Chill for 4-6 hours before eating.

Serve with melba toast or french bread

George Rogers

I like fish pie – whenever I have it I eat it all up because it's my favourite. I love apples. Sometimes I help mummy make cakes.

# smoked mackerel pâté

● **4 smoked mackerel fillets** ● **300g soft cream cheese** ● **1 lemon** ● **grated nutmeg** ● **freshly ground black pepper**

First skin the mackerel, chop roughly and place in a food processor. Add 300g cream cheese, the juice of half a lemon, a good pinch of grated nutmeg and freshly ground black pepper to taste. Once all these ingredients are in the food processor blend to a smooth paste. Then chill in the refrigerator for at least 30 minutes. Serve with melba toast and some salad leaves and cherry tomatoes.

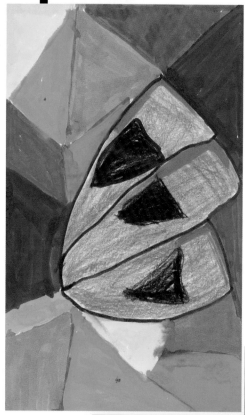

note
In the summer my dad catches mackerel and he smokes them in his home smoker. It is called a Little Chief Smoker and makes delicious smoked mackerel but, before he smokes the fish he cures them in a brine that is his own secret recipe, and he won't tell me because he says it's a secret.

Olivia Smith

My favourite foods are chicken and strawberries. I help my dad cook.

# mussels

**● 2 kg of mussels ● carrots ● leeks ● herbes de provence ● glass of dry white wine**

First clean the mussels and pull out the beards. (These are the stringy bits outside the mussel). Check every mussel and discard those that are open and do not close when you give them a firm tap on the worktop. Put a layer of mussels in a (mussel) pan, followed by a layer of chopped leeks and carrots. Add some herbes de provence. Continue with this layering until the pan is three quarters full. Add the glass of wine. Put a lid on the pan and cook the mussels until they have opened fully. This usually takes 5-7 minutes. Shake the pan carefully halfway through the cooking process. Serve with a garlic or mustard based dip and fresh bread.

Serves: 4

note

If you wish to serve this as a main meal, use 1kg of mussels per person and serve with chips!

Alec Gregory

I love pizzas and oranges. I help my mum make buns.

# prawn provençal

● **700g raw peeled tiger prawns** ● **700g tomatoes** ● **4 shallots or 1 small onion** ● **3 tbsp olive oil** ● **3 garlic cloves crushed or chopped** ● **1 level tbsp tomato paste** ● **150ml white wine** ● **bouquet garni** ● **salt & freshly ground black pepper**

Heat the olive oil in a large frying pan and add the finely chopped shallots. Cook for 1-2 minutes. Add the garlic and cook for only 30 seconds (do not allow the garlic to overcook). Then add the tomato paste and cook for a further minute. Now pour in the white wine, bring to the boil and simmer for about 5-10 minutes until very well reduced and syrupy. While the sauce is cooking peel, de-seed and chop the tomatoes. These can then be added to the mixture along with the bouquet garni and seasoning added to taste. Bring to the boil and cook very gently on the hob until pulpy. Finally add the raw seafood, return to the boil and simmer gently for 1-2 minutes until the prawns are pink and cooked through.

Serves: 6

note

Serve with crusty bread for a delicious starter or light lunch.

Laura Monk

I love pasta and mussels. My favourite fruit is mango. I enjoy helping mummy make the Christmas pudding.

# auntie joan's tuna dip

- 185g tin tuna chunks in brine or spring water
- 200g tub cream cheese – full or reduced fat
- salt and pepper ● 1 garlic clove ● tabasco sauce
- milk, plain yogurt, fresh lemon or lime juice

Beat the soft cheese in a bowl, drain the tuna and add to the cheese, add seasoning to taste and mix well using a wooden spoon. Add milk, yogurt, fresh lemon or lime juice to get the consistency required.

A tasty starter, snack or light supper to serve with toasted pitta bread, crudités or your favourite crisps, tortilla chips or breadsticks.

Emma &
James Davidson

Emma: My favourite food is toffee. At home I help do the washing up.
James: I love pizza and fruit salad. I make cups of tea for everyone and sometimes help mum.

# easy squid

- **500ml groundnut oil** ● **few pinches of sea salt** ● **few black peppercorns**
- **75g cornflour** ● **500g baby squid, cut into rings, tentacles unchopped** ● **I lemon**

Heat the oil in a frying pan over a high heat. Bash the salt and peppercorns in a pestle and mortar, or in a plastic bag with a rolling pin, until crushed.  Combine this mixture in a freezer bag with the cornflour. Add the squid and toss to coat lightly. When the oil is very hot fry the squid (knocking off any excess cornflour first) in batches and cook each batch for about a minute or so until crisp on the outside. Remove to plates lined with kitchen towel, leave to sit for half a minute, then remove the towel, squeeze over the lemon and serve immediately with a salad garnish.
Serves: 2

Jacob Wiseman

I like to eat chicken drumsticks. My favourite fruits are melon and oranges. I put the food on the table and clear away.

# mushroom and ham dip with crudités

- **1 packet of mushroom soup powder**
- **mushrooms – washed (about 6)** ● **ham**
- **500g double cream or crème fraiche**
- **carrots** ● **cucumber** ● **crisps**

dip

mushroom

Chop up the mushrooms and the ham into small

pieces.

Mix the soup powder in with the cream, add the

ham and mushrooms and stir together.

Chop the carrots and cucumber into strips.

Serve the dip in a bowl with the vegetables and

crisps around it.

carrot

cucumber

Sammy Hailey

I love pasta and

ketchup and making

cakes!

# tsatsiki

● **500g greek yogurt** ● **½ cucumber** ● **I clove garlic** ● **I tbsp extra virgin olive oil** ● **salt and pepper**

Grate the cucumber into
a colander and squeeze
out the juices.  Crush
or grate the garlic.  Add
the olive oil and salt and
pepper to the cucumber
and stir.  Stir in the
yogurt.

note
Serve with warm pitta bread.

Lucy & Eliza Tilbury
Eliza: My favourite
foods are treacle tart
and pomegranates. I
enjoy making pavlova
and crème brulee.
Lucy: I like pasta and
strawberries dipped in
chocolate. My job in
the kitchen is eating!!

# fajitas and daddy's quick guacamole

**Fajitas:**
- **250g chicken** ● **½ onion** ● **½ red pepper** ● **½ green pepper**
● **2 tbsp tomato puree** ● **I tbsp oil** ● **4 soft flour tortillas**

**Guacamole:**
● **I large avocado** ● **I heaped tbsp tomato puree** ● **juice from ½ lemon** ● **I heaped tsp brown sugar** ● **I clove garlic (chopped)** ● **I slice onion (finely chopped)** ● **tabasco to taste**

Thinly slice the chicken, onion and pepper. Stir fry chicken in a little oil until cooked. Add vegetables and tomato puree and stir fry for a further 1 – 2 minutes. Warm tortillas (10 seconds per tortilla).

Place guacamole ingredients in a blender, blitz and chill for 30 minutes. Construct the fajitas! Fill a tortilla with meat, vegetables and large dollops of guacamole. Fold/roll tortilla around filling and enjoy.

Luke Evans

My favourite food is chocolate...and I like carrots. I help mummy do the cooking.

# asparagus in ham

- **smoked ham** ● **whole asparagus**
- **grated cheese**

Roll each piece of asparagus in some ham and put
on an ovenproof tray. Grate some cheese on top
and put tray in the oven for 10-15 minutes.

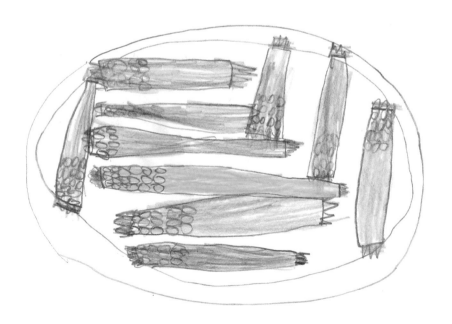

Jonathan Parr

I like to eat fish and
I like apples. I cook,
clear away my plate
and clear up after
everyone else.

# stuffed mushrooms

● **4 large field mushrooms** ● **4 rashers of bacon** ● **slice of bread** ● **1 cup grated cheddar cheese** ● **8 lettuce leaves**

Preheat oven to 180°C. Brush off the mushrooms and peel off any loose skin. Remove the stalks from the mushrooms and put them on one side. Put the bread in a blender and turn into breadcrumbs. Add the bacon and mushroom stalks to the blender and mix with the breadcrumbs. Spread the mixture evenly between the 4 mushrooms. Place on a baking tray and cook in the centre of the oven for 20 minutes. After 20 minutes place the cheese on top of the mushrooms and leave them in the oven for a further 5 minutes. Place the stuffed mushrooms on a bed of lettuce and serve.

Serves: 4

Georgia-Kit Penrose

My favourite food is ice cream.

# ciabatta with spinach and brie melt

- **8 slices of ciabatta bread**
- **220g fresh baby spinach leaves** ● **4 tbsp olive oil**
- **8 tbsp cranberry sauce** ● **110g brie, sliced thinly** ● **salt & freshly ground pepper**

Toast bread under a hot grill. Meanwhile, briskly cook the spinach in a saucepan with the olive oil for 1-2 minutes or until the leaves just wilt. Season with salt & pepper and drain thoroughly. Spread the cranberry sauce over the slices of toast. Spoon the spinach on top and finally arrange the slices of brie over the spinach. Flash under a hot grill for 1-2 minutes or until the cheese just starts to melt. Serve immediately.

Serves: 4

Emma Green

I like mummy's roast dinner and carrots and apples. Sometimes I set the table for our meal.

marvellous

mains

# teddy bear's burgers

- **1kg minced beef** ● **2 medium red onions chopped finely**
- **2 eggs** ● **1-2 handfuls of fresh breadcrumbs** ● **1 heaped tsp dijon mustard** ● **salt & black pepper** ● **optional: tsp ground coriander and/or tsp ground cumin**

Preheat the oven to 230°C/450°F. Mix and scrunch all the ingredients together, add as many breadcrumbs as you need to bind the mixture together without it getting too dry. Divide into 4 then roll into balls and flatten a little bit. Put in the oven and cook for 25 minutes.

Serves: 4

Ella Bean

I like chinese food. At home I help bake cakes.

note

Serve in a bun, with some salad and maybe potato wedges or fries.

# cornish pasties

● **200g plain flour** ● **100g butter** ● **200g rump steak** ● **1 small carrot** ● **1 small potato** ● **1 onion** ● **5ml dried mixed herbs** ● **1 egg**

Sift the flour into a bowl, then cube and rub in the fat until it resembles fine breadcrumbs. Add 30ml water, mix to a smooth dough and leave to rest for 20 minutes. Preheat the oven to 200°C/400°F/Gas Mark 6. Finely dice the beef, peel and dice the carrot, onion and potato. Mix together in a bowl with the mixed herbs. Roll out the pasty and cut four 15cm (6in) circles. Place spoonfuls of the filling in the middle of each pasty. Beat egg and brush the edges. Bring together the edges, crimping to seal. Make a small slit on the side to let the steam out. Place on a lightly oiled greaseproof paper on a baking sheet. Brush with beaten egg and cook for 35-40 minutes until golden and cooked through.

Serves: 4

Reece & Sophie Burgess

I love chocolate. I help mummy and daddy in the kitchen.

# chicken and kiwi

● **4 chicken breasts (skinned & diced)** ● **4 large carrots**
● **6 kiwis** ● **4 spring onions** ● **2 heaped tsp caster**
**sugar** ● **6 tbsp sweet white wine** ● **3 tbsp lime juice**

Peel and chop the carrots into batons. Peel the kiwis and cut them in half. Slice each half into quarters. Top and tail the spring onions, remove the outer skin and slice diagonally. Heat a tablespoon of olive oil in a large frying pan. Add a tablespoon of lime juice with the chicken pieces to the frying pan and brown all over until cooked. Drain off the waste from the frying pan, place the chicken pieces on a plate and keep warm for later use. Wipe out the large frying pan using a paper towel, add a tablespoon of olive oil and heat. Add the carrots and spring onions and cook for 2 minutes. Add the caster sugar, wine and lime juice to the frying pan and bring to the boil for 2 minutes. Return the chicken to the frying pan and add the kiwi. Cook for a further 2 minutes.
Serves: 4

note

Best served with cous cous.

Matt Burnard

My favourite food is chicken with kiwi! I like peas. In the kitchen I help cut up the vegetables.

# sausage toad

**● 80g plain flour ● I free range egg ● 100ml water ● 100ml milk ● 8 sausages (butchers homemade chipolatas) ● splash of olive oil**

Sieve flour into a bowl.  Add egg and then mix milk and water slowly in until you have a smooth mixture.  Preheat oven to 200°C/400°F/Gas Mark 6.  Put a large glass casserole dish with a splash of olive oil in the oven.  After ¾ minutes remove and put in sausages and cover with batter mix.  Cook for 25-30 minutes until batter is crispy.  Serve with mashed potatoes, carrots and peas.

Serves: 4

Tegan Chapman

I love chocolate, roast chicken and tomatoes. Mum and dad cook and I help a little bit but sometimes I watch.

# chicken with creamy bacon penne

- 1 tbsp olive oil ● 2 boneless, skinless chicken breasts
- 100g smoked lardons (chopped bacon)
- 4 tbsp dry white wine ● 100g frozen petits pois (small peas)
- 5 tbsp double cream ● 220g pack "instant" cooked penne

Heat the oil in a deep frying pan and add the chicken breasts. Leave to cook over a high heat for 4 minutes while you gather other ingredients together. Turn the chicken over in the pan then add the wine and leave to bubble over a high heat until it is virtually evaporated. Add the peas, cream, pasta and season. Stir well, cover the pan and cook for 4 minutes until the chicken is cooked through.

Serves: 2

note

This amazingly quick and tasty dish works well with fresh salmon too – just cook for 3 minutes on each side and leave out the bacon.

Eleanor Hill

My favourite food is curry and I love raspberries. In the kitchen I like to do some baking.

# sausage and baked bean hotpot

**● 8 quorn sausages ● ½ onion ● 2 tins baked beans ● cheese ● 8 potatoes ● garlic clove**

Chop and fry onion in light oil and remove when golden. Chop sausages and fry in light oil until they are golden. Chop a garlic clove and add to sausage. Add cooked onion and 2 tins of baked beans and heat. Boil potatoes until soft. Place sausage and beans in an oven dish. Chop the cooked potatoes and place on top, add salt, pepper and cheese and place in oven for 45 minutes on Gas Mark 5. Serves:  4

Ben Parsons

I like to eat sausage and bean hotpot and chicken madras. In the kitchen I like cooking spaghetti bolognese and pancakes.

# chicken in black bean sauce

- 900g un-skinned chicken breasts ● 2 tbsp light soy sauce
● 2 tbsp rice wine ● olive oil ● I tbsp finely chopped fresh ginger ● I tbsp finely chopped garlic ● 450g jar of black bean sauce ● 75ml chicken stock

Cut chicken pieces into 5cm chunks. Mix soy sauce and rice wine and pour over chicken pieces. Marinade for at least 10 minutes then drain and discard marinade. Heat wok, add oil and when hot add ginger. Stir fry for a few seconds and add garlic. Add chicken and stir fry for 5 minutes until brown. Add stock and black bean sauce. Reduce heat and simmer for 5 minutes. Serve hot with noodles and peas.

Serves: 6-8

Lyndsay-Jean Smith

I love salmon. At home I enjoy making onion dumplings.

# eyeballs in blood

**Eyeballs:** ● **250g minced pork** ● **250g minced beef** ● **1 egg**
● **1 tsp oregano** ● **1 clove of garlic, minced** ● **3 tbsp semolina**
● **salt and black pepper**
**Blood sauce:** ● **1 onion** ● **2 cloves of garlic** ● **1 tsp oregano** ● **1 tbsp butter**
● **1 tbsp olive oil** ● **700g tomato passata** ● **pinch of sugar** ● **100ml full fat milk**

Put everything in a large bowl and mix with your hands,
very yucky, lovely, then shape the mixture with your
hands into small balls (about the size of an eyeball). Chill in
the fridge. Put onion, garlic and oregano in processor and
blitz to a pulp. Heat the butter and oil in a large pan, add
the onion mixture and cook for 10 minutes. Add passata,
half fill the empty jar with water and add to pan with rest
of ingredients. Pop the eyeballs into blood sauce and cook
for 20 minutes. Serve with pasta of choice.

Serves: 4

Lloyd Vosper

I like spaghetti
bolognese and mango.
Sometimes I do some
cooking.

# chicken fillets with mango chutney and apricot

- **2 chicken breasts** ● **1 tbsp apricot jam** ● **1 tbsp mango chutney**
- **3 tbsp mayonnaise** ● **1 tsp worcestershire sauce** ● **1 tbsp lemon juice**

Mix all the ingredients together for the sauce.  Put the chicken into a small ovenproof dish, pour over the sauce and cover the dish with aluminium foil. Bake in the oven, preheated to 180°C/350°F/Gas Mark 4 for 30 minutes.

Serves: 2-3

William Trinder

I like to eat spaghetti bolognese.

# bacon wrapped chicken breasts

- **4 chicken breasts** ● **4 slices cheese (cheddar or whatever you prefer)** ● **4 rashers bacon** ● **50g butter** ● **olive oil**

Flatten chicken breasts.  Place slice of cheese inside,

wrap bacon around.  Line an oven dish with tinfoil,

dot chicken breasts with butter and a dash of oil.

Cook in oven at 180°C/350°F/Gas Mark 4 for an hour

or until ready.

Serves: 4

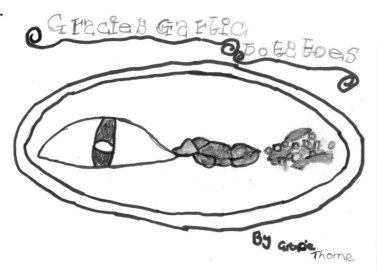

Gracies Garlic Potatoes

By Gracie Thorne

note
Great with garlic potatoes and vegetables of your choice.

Gracie Thorne

I love fruit salad! In the kitchen...I eat....lots of....fruit salad!

# stuffed potatoes twice baked

● **4 baking potatoes** ● **butter or margarine**
● **salt and pepper** ● **chives**

Preheat the oven to Gas Mark 7 (425°F/220°C). Wash and dry the potatoes, prick the skins all over with a fork.  Place them in the oven for up to one and a half hours. Take the potatoes out of the oven, cut them in half and leave them to cool.  Scoop the middle out of the potatoes and put into a bowl.  Add in your favourite filling and mash into the potato, add salt and pepper if desired.  Fill the potato skins with the mixture.  Place the potato back in the oven to reheat. Serve with salad.

Serves: 4

Suggested fillings: cream cheese and chives, tuna and sweetcorn

Catriona Mackay

I love gammon roast and cauliflower cheese. I enjoy cooking spaghetti bolognese.

# ham and potato gratin

● **30ml olive oil** ● **I onion, chopped** ● **I clove garlic, crushed** ● **125g thickly sliced ham, cut into pieces** ● **2 eggs** ● **300ml milk** ● **100g cheddar cheese** ● **salt and pepper** ● **450g potatoes, peeled**

Heat the oil in a frying pan, add the onion and garlic and cook gently for 10 minutes. Remove from the heat and stir in the ham. Whisk the eggs and milk in a bowl. Stir in the grated cheese and season with salt and pepper. Grate the potatoes coarsely into a separate bowl, squeeze out as much liquid as possible and stir the potato into the egg mixture. Add the ham and onion and mix thoroughly. Turn the mixture into a buttered gratin dish. Place in a preheated oven 190°C/375°/Gas Mark 5 for 35 – 40 minutes. Finish off by browning under the grill if necessary.

Serves: 4

Robert Meheux

I like to eat meatballs and brussel sprouts. At home mummy cooks lots and daddy woks the noodles!

# garlic and mushroom mash

**● potatoes ● mushrooms ● garlic butter ● parsley ● ½ tsp salt ● dash of ground pepper ● dash of milk**

Chop some mushrooms, clean them and finely chop again.  Fry on a low heat in garlic butter and add fresh parsley.  Steam the potatoes and season them using ½ teaspoon of sea salt, a dash of pepper (ground) mashed together with 100g of garlic butter and a dash of milk.

This American dish brings a smile to a lot of people.  It is a delicious side plate addition to any meal.

Tricia & Molly McCarth[...]

Molly: I love chocolate and apples. At home [...] help make tea.

Tricia: My favourite foods are chocolate and salad. I help in the kitchen by......
eating everything in the cupboards!

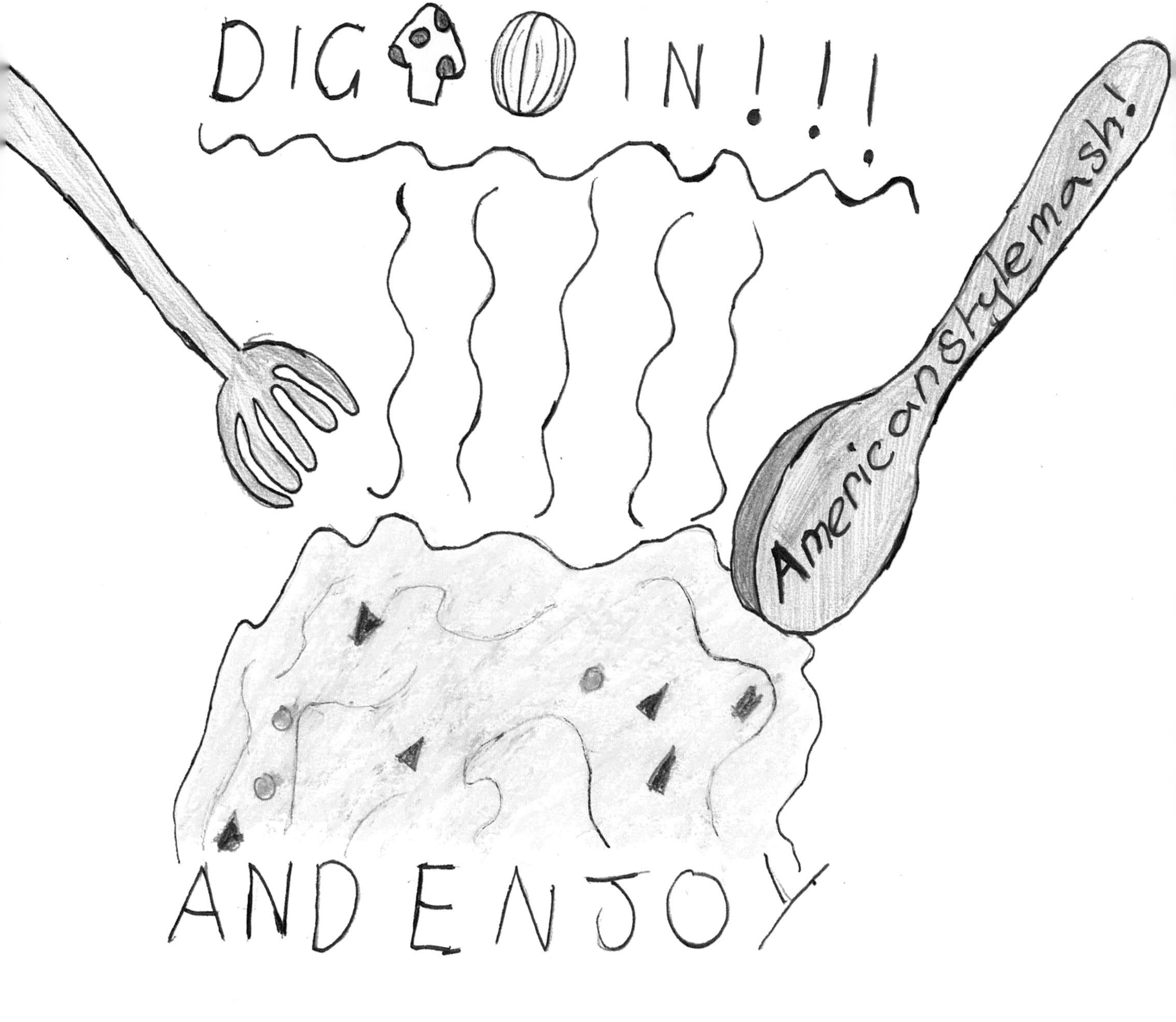
DIG IN!!!
Americanstylemash!
AND ENJOY

# leek and bacon mash

● **675g potatoes** ● **4 rashers of bacon** ● **1 medium leek** ● **150ml semi-skimmed milk** ● **grated cheese**

Peel and cut potatoes into small chunks, cook, drain and return to pan. Grill bacon and chop roughly. Slice leeks finely and fry until golden brown. Boil the milk then pour over the potatoes and mash. Add the bacon and leek to the potatoes. Sprinkle with grated cheese and brown under the grill.

Anna &
William Snawdon

I like pasta and apples. In the kitchen I help by cutting vegetables and fruit with mum.

# spaghetti carbonara

● **450g spaghetti** ● **25g butter** ● **225g smoked ham, diced**
● **3 eggs, beaten** ● **300ml double cream** ● **50g grated parmesan cheese** ● **salt and black pepper**

Cook pasta in boiling salted water, following instructions on packet. While pasta is cooking, melt butter in a large pan. Add the ham to the pan. Cook for 5 minutes stirring occasionally, until slightly brown. Beat together the eggs, cream and salt and pepper until well blended. Add to the pan and cook for 2 minutes, stirring constantly or until the mixture begins to thicken but not scramble. Add parmesan cheese and cook for a further minute. Drain the pasta well and turn into a large, warmed bowl. Pour over sauce and mix thoroughly. Scatter with chopped fresh parsley to garnish.

Serves: 4

Rebecca Teale

My favourite food is spaghetti carbonara. I like cabbage as well. At home I help make hot chocolate.

# country-style bolognese

● I tbsp oil ● I onion, chopped ● I garlic clove, chopped
● I stick celery, chopped ● I carrot, peeled and chopped
● 500g minced beef ● 400g can chopped tomatoes ● I tbsp tomato
puree ● 150ml beef stock ● 225g long spaghetti ● basil leaves to
garnish ● 50g parmesan cheese, grated

Heat oil in a frying pan, add onion, garlic and vegetables
and cook until softened. Add minced beef and fry
until browned. Add tomatoes, puree and stock and
bring to the boil. Season, cover and simmer for 25
minutes, stirring occasionally. Bring a large pan of lightly
salted water to the boil, add dry spaghetti and cook.
Drain spaghetti and mix meat mixture together with
pasta and serve. Garnish with basil leaves and grated
parmesan.

Serves: 4

Thomas Burt

I love chips and I
also like bananas.
Sometimes I help
feed my baby
brother.

# yummy pasta sauce

- 1 carton italian passata with garlic and herbs
- 4 tbsp dark soy sauce • 2 tbsp sweet chilli sauce • 1 crushed garlic clove • 6 button mushrooms • 6 cherry tomatoes
- 75g extra lean smoked bacon
- 2 sausages • ½ tsp season of all seasoning • pasta

In a medium sized frying pan cook chopped bacon thoroughly, add cut up sausages and cook for a few minutes. Add the mushrooms using a little oil if required. When mushrooms are almost cooked add seasoning and tomatoes and cook for 1 minute. Turn off the stove and leave to stand. In a microwavable bowl pour in passata, chilli sauce, soy, garlic and sweetener and microwave for 1 minute. Add sauce to pan and simmer for 1 minute before adding to cooked pasta.

Paige Parsons

My favourite food is cottage pie and I like pineapple. I help clean up in the kitchen.

# perfect pasta

- **250g pasta shapes** ● **¼ teaspoon salt**
- **55g butter** ● **40g plain flour** ● **450ml milk**
- **125g cheddar cheese, grated**
- **125g ham, roughly chopped** ● **4 cherry tomatoes** cut into quarters ● **salt and freshly ground black pepper** ● **25g parmesan cheese, grated**

Preheat the oven to 200°C /Gas mark 6. Heat some water in the large saucepan. Add salt and bring to boil then add the pasta carefully taking care not to splash. Cook the pasta according to the pack instructions. Gently melt the butter in a saucepan over a low heat. Add the flour and mix well, cook the mixture for 1 minute. Stir in the milk a little at a time to make a smooth sauce. Put pan back on heat, stir while the sauce thickens. When the sauce boils, turn down the heat and cook, stirring for 1-2 minutes. Remove from heat, mix in cheddar, ham and tomatoes. Season. Drain the pasta and mix with the sauce. Place in ovenproof dish and sprinkle with parmesan and bake in oven on a baking tray for 20-25 minutes.

Serves: 4

Joshua Thomasson Some of my favourite foods are tagliatelle and strawberries. I like making fresh tagliatelle and decorating food and cakes.

# cheesy tuna pasta

● **100g butter** ● **75g plain flour** ● **350ml milk** ● **125g grated cheese** ● **300g pasta [any shape]** ● **185g tuna in spring water** ● **250g sweetcorn [tinned or frozen]**

Cook the pasta in plenty of water. Make the cheese sauce, melt the butter in a saucepan, add the flour and blend together. Add the milk slowly to make a smooth sauce and then add the grated cheese. Drain the pasta and return it to the saucepan. Add the cheese sauce, tuna and sweetcorn mixture to the pasta and mix together.

Serves: 4

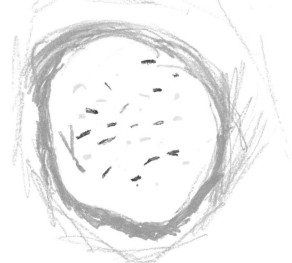

Georgia Towl

My favourite food is salmon.

note

Serve either by itself or with a side salad and crusty bread.

# fishy pesto pasta

**For the pesto:**
● **4 garlic cloves** ● **3 tbsp grated parmesan**
● **150g extra virgin olive oil** ● **75g fresh basil** ● **125g pine nuts** ● **salt and pepper to taste**
**For the fish:**
● **4 pieces white fish, i.e. haddock** ● **200g cherry tomatoes** ● **200g chestnut mushrooms**
● **300g pasta**

Preheat oven to 200°C/400°F/Gas Mark 6. Blend pesto ingredients in a food processor (set aside). Place each piece of fish on a piece of tin foil, large enough to wrap in a parcel. Smear the fish generously with pesto sauce. Halve the tomatoes and mushrooms. Arrange around the fish and place on top, add a sprig of thyme. Wrap the fish into a parcel, keeping a small hole in the centre. Bake for 20 – 25 minutes on a baking tray in centre of oven. Cook and drain pasta, toss in olive oil, add salt and pepper to taste.

Serves: 4

Serve fish on a bed of pasta with tomatoes and mushrooms. Pour remaining liquid over the pasta.

Charlie Hurley-Smit

My favourite foods are pasta and sweetcorn. In the kitchen I help with the washing up.

# tuna fish cakes

- **5 potatoes** ● **1 tbsp butter** ● **2 tbsp milk**
- **1 tin tuna fish** ● **1 tin sweetcorn**
- **fresh parsley** ● **breadcrumbs**
- **salt and pepper**

Boil potatoes until soft then mash with butter and
milk. Add tuna fish, sweetcorn, parsley and salt and
pepper. Divide mixture into ten portions and coat
with breadcrumbs. Place under grill until golden.

Serves: Makes 10 cakes

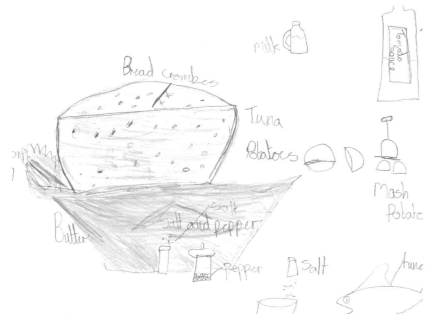

William Hodge

I like tomatoes and
melon. At home I help
with the washing up.

# easy grilled salmon fillets

- **4 medium sized salmon fillets**
- **soy sauce** ● **vinegar** ● **fresh herbs: rosemary, sage, oregano** ● **freshly ground black pepper** ● **butter or margarine**

Wash the fillets in cold water and then dry them off with kitchen towel. Place them on a foil-covered grill tray. Sprinkle on a generous amount of soy sauce and vinegar. Chop up the herbs very finely (use dried if you wish), then sprinkle evenly over each fillet. Add a little black pepper and then two or three blobs of margarine or butter on each fillet. Place under a medium grill until the tops are golden brown and crispy.

Serves: 4

note
The soy sauce gives a lovely oriental flavour and there is no need to add any salt.

Nina Folland

I like noodles. I help at home by putting chocolate on the pancakes.

# crispy fried cod fillets with tartare sauce

- **4 cod fillets weighing about 100g each**
- **40g dried breadcrumbs ● salt and pepper**
- **1 egg ● 1tbsp vegetable oil ● tartare sauce**
- **lemon wedges**

Cut the fish into 3cm wide strips. In a shallow bowl mix the breadcrumbs and seasoning. Beat the egg. Dip the fish into the egg and then in the breadcrumbs. Heat oil in a frying pan, add fish and fry gently for about 8 minutes turning half way through. Garnish with lemon wedges and serve with tartare sauce.

Serves: 4

note
These are really nice with homemade potato wedges and broccoli or peas.

Jack Castles

I love ice cream and nectarines. When my mum makes me I help in the kitchen.

# prawn stir-fry

- 100g baby sweetcorn ● 100g carrots
- 22.5ml vegetable oil ● 2 spring onions
- 100g sugar snap peas or mangetout
- 250ml chicken stock ● 15ml soy sauce ● 30ml sherry
or sake ● 2 tbsp cornflour ● 225g cooked king prawns

Halve the sweetcorn lengthways, then cut across in half again.  Using a potato peeler, cut thin strips from the carrot and cut these in half again, to make long thin, curly strips of carrot.  Heat the oil in a frying pan or wok and sauté the spring onion for 1 minute.  Add the other vegetables and stir fry for 2-3 minutes.  Remove the vegetables and set aside.  Mix together the chicken stock, soy sauce, sherry and cornflour.  Pour the mixture into the frying pan and stir constantly while bringing to the boil.  Reduce the heat and simmer, stirring for 1 or 2 minutes until thickened.  Stir in the prawns and the vegetables and heat through.

Serves: 4

Mia O'Daly

My favourite things to eat are biscuits.

# salmon fishcakes

- **800g skinless salmon fillets** ● **500ml milk**
- **600g potatoes, peeled and chopped into chunks**
- **4 tbsp natural yogurt** ● **I tsp mustard**
- **200g sweetcorn** ● **flour for dusting** ● **I egg, beaten**
- **100g breadcrumbs** ● **4 tbsp vegetable oil** ● **vegetables to serve**

Place the salmon in a pan, cover with milk and simmer for 5–10 minutes. Remove the salmon and put on a plate. Flake into large pieces with a fork and leave to cool. Cook the potatoes over a low heat, drain then mash. Stir the yogurt, mustard and sweetcorn into the mash and season. Mix the fish with the mash. Dust your hands and work surface with flour and shape the mixture into cakes. Dip the cakes into the egg then cover in breadcrumbs. Fry the fishcakes until each side is golden.

note
Serve with vegetables and enjoy!

Izabel &
Tommy Brown

Some of my favourite foods are salmon and bananas. At home I like to do some cooking with mummy.

# paella

● **2 chicken thighs, 2 breasts, 2 drumsticks** ● **flour to dust chicken** ● **salt and pepper** ● **olive oil** ● **1 chorizo sausage sliced diagonally ¼ inch thick** ● **6 slices pancetta** ● **1 onion, finely chopped** ● **4 cloves garlic finely chopped** ● **2 -3 large pinches saffron** ● **3½ pints chicken stock** ● **1 heaped tsp smoked paprika** ● **500g paella rice** ● **1 small bunch flat-leafed parsley, chopped** ● **handful peas** ● **500g mussels** ● **8 – 10 large prawns, shell and veins removed** ● **2 small squid, trimmed, gutted and cut into small pieces** ● **1 lemon cut into wedges**

Preheat oven to 190°C/375°F/Gas Mark 5. Cut breast in half and remove joints off legs. Dust chicken with seasoned flour. In a large flat pan fry the thighs and drumsticks in the olive oil until brown, remove from pan and continue to cook them in the oven for 30 minutes. Put the saffron in a little hot stock. Brown off the chicken breast, add chorizo and pancetta. Once crisp, reduce the heat. Add onion and garlic until soft. Pour in the saffron and some stock into the pan. Add the paprika and rice and stir continuously. If rice needs stock keep adding until cooked. Add peas, mussels, prawns, squid, thighs and drumsticks. Add the parsley and place the lemon around the pan and serve.

Serves: 6

Emily Mills

I like lasagne, strawberries and bananas. At home I like helping mummy make biscuits and muffins.

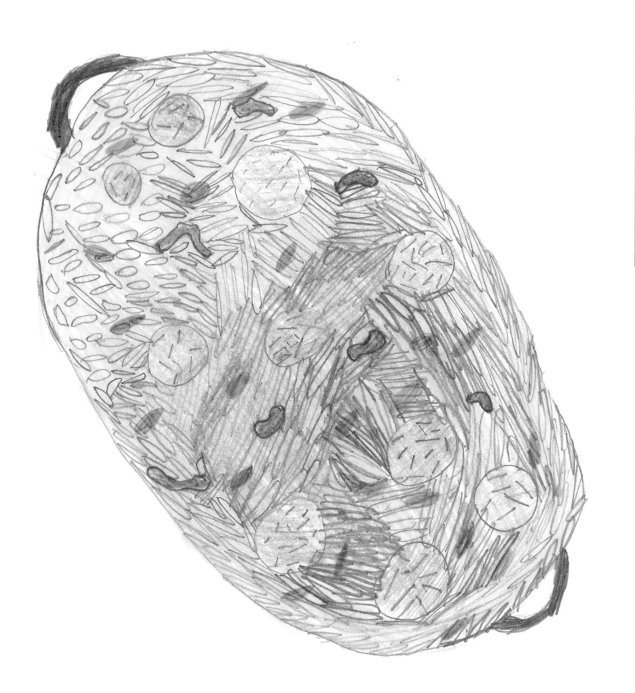

# billy's fishy leekie pie

- 1 bag new potatoes ● 2 salmon fillets ● 1 leek
- cup of frozen peas ● cup of small broccoli
florets ● 50g plain flour ● 50g butter ● 1 pint milk
- 1 tbsp fresh pesto

Boil potatoes until soft, crush with a fork and set aside.

Poach salmon fillets in milk until fish changes colour.

Transfer fish into pie dish and flake, save milk for sauce.

Add butter until melted then add flour until it forms a

paste.  Slowly add milk until sauce thickens.  When thick

add tablespoon of pesto.  In a separate frying pan cook

leeks in butter until soft.  Add all other vegetables and

cook for a few minutes.  Add to fish dish.  Cover with

sauce and put potatoes on top with knob of butter.  Put

into hot oven for 25 minutes.

Serves: 3

Billy Lloyd

My favourite food

is pasta pesto and

I like kiwi fruit. At

home I help ice the

fairy cakes.

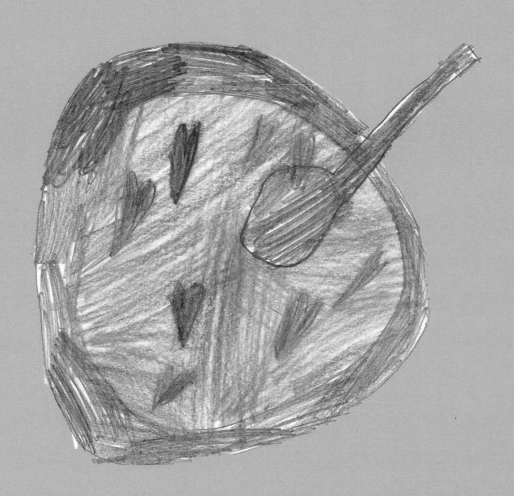

# apple in and out

● **225g self raising flour** ● **100g shredded suet** ● **50g caster sugar** ● **pinch of salt** ● **2 large cooking apples peeled, cored and cut into chunky pieces** ● **cold water to mix**

Preheat oven to Gas Mark 4/350°F/180°C. Mix dry ingredients together in a bowl and stir in the prepared apples. Add just enough water to form a soft but not sticky dough. Put into pie dish, spread out and bake for approximately 45 minutes until golden brown in colour.

Serves: 4

Joshua Bath
My favourite food is pizza and I like red grapes. In the kitchen I cook pizza with ham and mushrooms!

# festive fruit sundaes

- **290g can raspberries in apple juice**
- **100g strawberries, hulled and sliced ● 2 kiwi fruit, peeled and sliced ● 500ml tub vanilla ice-cream**
- **To decorate:**
- **12 raspberries ● 4 mint sprigs**

Drain raspberries and set aside 2 tbsp juice. Mash the raspberries with a fork, blender or food processor until smooth and runny. Using a spoon, press raspberries through a fine sieve into a small bowl. Discard seeds from sieve. Stir reserved juice into raspberry puree. Using half of the strawberries put equal quantities into 4 tall dessert glasses. Cover with half the kiwi fruit and spoon 2 scoops of ice-cream on top of the fruit in each glass. Carefully drizzle the raspberry puree over the ice-cream. Arrange the remaining strawberry slices, kiwi fruit and fresh raspberries around the side of the puree. Decorate each sundae with a mint sprig and serve immediately.

Serves: Makes 4 sundaes

Anastasia &
Angelina Benson

Angelina: I like cheesy chips. Plums are lovely too! I help wash up.

Anastasia: My favourite meal is sausages and chips. I like strawberries as well.

# summer fruit pudding

- **225g redcurrants** • **110g blackcurrants**
- **450g raspberries** • **150g caster sugar**
- **7-8 slices of white bread**

Place the fruits and sugar in a large saucepan over a medium heat and let them cook for about 3 – 5 minutes until the sugar has dissolved and the juices begin to run. Remove the fruit from the heat. Line a small pudding basin with the bread, overlapping them and sealing well by pressing the edges together. Fill in any gaps with small pieces of bread so that no juice can get through when you add the fruit. Pour the fruit and juice in (except for about two thirds of a cupful) then cover the pudding with another slice of bread. Place a small plate or saucer on top and place a weight on it and leave in fridge overnight. Just before serving turn pudding out onto a large serving dish and spoon the reserved juice all over to soak any bits of bread that still look white.

note
Serve cut into wedges with a dollop of thick cream.

Sophie Broughton

I love pasta and melon. In the kitchen I like to bake cakes.

# apple snowballs

- **4 medium cooking apples**
- **110g caster sugar** ● **2 tbsp sugar** ● **2tbsp mincemeat**

Peel and core apples, stuff with mincemeat and sugar.
Bake in oven for 30-40 minutes until tender but not soft.
Make meringue by whisking egg whites until stiff and
fold in sugar with a spoon. When apples are cool cover
with meringue. Decorate with cherries and bake in the
oven until meringue slightly browns.

Serves: 4

Hannah Carroll

I like chinese food. I help
at home by putting
things on the tray.

# strudel

● **puff pastry** ● **english summer fruits from your garden, e.g. raspberries, strawberries, blackberries or apples** ● **milk** ● **sugar**

Roll out two identical pieces of pastry. Place fruit on one piece. Make slits in the other piece of pastry 1cm in from each side and each end. Place the piece with slits on top. Press down all around the edge of the pastry with the top of a spoon to seal your strudel. Brush a little milk over the pastry and sprinkle with a little sugar if desired. Bake at 180°C/350°F/Gas Mark 4 for 25 minutes or until golden

note
Serve with custard or ice-cream.

Ben Chapman

I love sausage toad and potatoes. I do the dishwashing.

# banana split

● **two bananas** ● **one large packet of chocolate buttons** ● **one metre of tin foil**

First cut each banana in half, but making sure that it is still joined.  Next put evenly spaced chocolate buttons inside the banana.  Put it in the microwave for 1 minute and 30 seconds.  Finally carefully lift out your banana splits and enjoy!

Lawrence Ellerton

My favourite food is chocolate and my favourite healthy food is...chocolate cake! In the kitchen I make a mess and lick the chocolate bowl!

# rocking raspberry shortcake

● **160g self-raising flour** ● **60g butter**
● **60g caster sugar** ● **½ tsp nutmeg** ● **raspberries**

First rub the flour and butter together then mix in the sugar. Press half the mixture into a small loose-based greased cake tin. Put the raspberries in the tin and the rest of the mixture on top. Pat down firmly.

Put into a preheated oven (200°C/400°F/Gas Mark 6) for 30-35mins, when a knife comes out clean it is ready. Stand for 5 minutes, loosen sides and turn out on to a plate. Dust with icing sugar and serve with cream.

Serves: 6

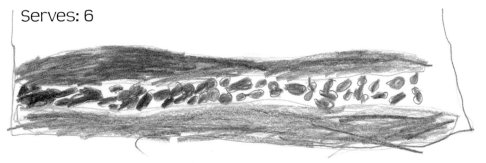

Top tip – if you haven't got any raspberries try delicious blackcurrants, gooseberries, strawberries or even rhubarb!!

Sam Parr

I love roast dinners and oranges. I normally set the table for me and my brother.

# strawberry meringues

- **2 large free range egg whites**
- **110g unrefined caster sugar ● double cream for whipping ● fresh strawberries**

Preheat the oven to 140°C/275°F/Gas Mark 1.
Line a baking tray with non-stick baking paper.
Place the egg whites in a large bowl and begin
whisking, continue until the egg whites stand up
in stiff peaks.  Whisk the sugar in a spoonful at
a time until you have a stiff and glossy mixture.
Spoon ten rounds of mixture onto the baking
tray and place in the centre of the oven for 1
hour.  Turn the oven off and leave the meringues
to dry out in the oven until completely cold. Whip
the cream, wash, hull and slice the strawberries
then arrange on top of the meringue rounds.

Olivia Wiseman

My favourite food
is spaghetti with
meatballs. I like apples
as well. I enjoy baking
cakes with my mum.

# apple and orange crumble

- **700g cooking apples, peeled, cored and sliced** ● **grated rind and juice of 1 orange** ● **25g light soft brown sugar**
- **100g plain flour** ● **50g plain wholemeal flour**
- **75g butter** ● **40g icing sugar, sieved**
- **1.25ml ground cinnamon**

Put the apples, orange rind and juice and sugar into a 4 litre ovenproof serving dish. Put the flours into a mixing bowl and rub in the butter until the mixture resembles fine breadcrumbs. Stir in the icing sugar and cinnamon, making sure all the ingredients are thoroughly combined. Sprinkle the crumble topping over the apple. Bake at 200°C/400°F/Gas Mark 6 for 30-40 minutes until the topping is crisp and golden.

note
Serve with fresh cream or hot custard.

Byrony Green - picture by Harriet Wright & Olivia Ellis

I like roast chicken and bananas. In the kitchen I like eating yogurts!

# tart tatin

- **3 crisp juicy apples** ● **125g butter**
- **150g brown sugar** ● **I pack puff pastry**

Core and slice the apples into segment shapes, arrange the slices in circles around the frying pan until the pan is covered. Add small knobs of butter evenly around the pan and then sprinkle on the sugar. Put the pan on a medium heat and cook the mixture until the butter and sugar have melted. DO NOT STIR AS YOU WILL RUIN THE CIRCULAR PATTERN OF THE APPLES. Once the mix has melted and browned take the pan off the heat. Roll out enough pastry to cover the pan and trim around the edge with a sharp knife. Then pat down the pastry. Put the pan in an oven at 180°C/350°F/Gas Mark 4 and leave until the pastry is brown and cooked. Put the pan in a cool place and when the whole mix is cold put a large serving plate over the pan and turn it upside down.

Dougal McDonald

I love pizza and fruit salad. At home I sometimes make cakes.

# a little bit of what you fancy pancakes!

- 110g plain flour
- 1 large egg (beaten)
- 1 tbsp oil
- 300ml milk
- pinch of salt

Sift the flour into a bowl and add a pinch of salt. Make a well in the flour and add the egg and milk gradually, mixing well. Leave the mixture to stand for half an hour. Add the oil to a frying pan and heat. Once hot, add spoonfuls of mixture until the pan is covered by a thin layer. When the mixture starts bubbling, turn the pancake over by tossing in the air – don't forget to catch it! Once cooked, transfer to a plate and add a little bit of what you fancy! (e.g. maple syrup, sugar, jam, cheese, strawberries

Serves: Makes 12 pancakes

Callum Green

I love rice cakes. In the kitchen I help by making cakes.

# upside down pudding

- 55g butter or margarine ● 55g caster sugar ● 1 medium egg ● 85g self-raising flour ● 25g butter or margarine ● 25g light brown sugar ● 1 small tin mandarin oranges, peaches or pineapple or chopped up fresh fruit ● glace cherries

Grease a 7inch sandwich tin with the butter or margarine. Sprinkle the greased tin evenly with the sugar. Open the tin of fruit and drain off the juice. Lay the drained fruit in the tin until it is completely covered, putting glace cherries where desired. Set aside while you mix the pudding.

Cream together the butter and sugar until smooth. Add the egg and beat well. Stir in the flour, add a little of the reserved juice if the mix is dry or stiff. Spoon the pudding mixture carefully over the fruit and smooth over the top. Cook at 180°C/350°F/Gas Mark 4 for about 20 – 25 minutes until firm to touch and golden brown. Remove from oven and allow to cool before turning out onto a plate.

note
Serve hot or cold with or without custard.

Sophie Highfield

I like to eat pizza and apples. At mealtimes I make the cold drinks.

# iced raspberry mousse

● **150g raspberries** ● **4 tbsp icing sugar, sifted** ● **4 tbsp greek-style yogurt** ● **150ml double cream** ● **meringues** ● **mint leaves to decorate**

Mash the raspberries in a bowl then add sugar. Stir raspberries and sugar together then add yogurt and mix again. Pour in cream and whisk until thick and points appear when whisk lifted. Add to yogurt and gently mix with spoon. Carry on until whole mixture is pink. Break the meringues into small pieces and add to mixture, stirring them in. Spoon mixture into dishes and leave in freezer for 2 hours. Take out and decorate with a raspberry and 2 mint leaves.

Serves: 4

Eathan & Jasmine Nisbett

Eathan: I like chips. My favourite vegetables are carrots. Sometimes I help set the table.

# lucia's summer pie

- 10 plain chocolate digestive biscuits ● 1½ level tbsp caster sugar ● 50g butter or margarine ● For the filling: ● 1 small tin of sweetened condensed milk ● 125ml (¼ pint) double cream ● 100g strawberries ● 1 kiwi fruit ● 2 lemons

Crush the biscuits with a rolling pin, place crumbs in a mixing bowl and add the sugar. Melt the butter in a saucepan over a low heat, remove from heat and stir in the biscuit mixture. Mix well and spoon into the centre of the pie plate. Using the back of a tablespoon press the mixture over the base and around the sides of the dish to make a crust. Chill in the fridge for an hour. Place the condensed milk and cream into a mixing basin. Finely grate the rind of 1 lemon. Squeeze the juice from 2 lemons and strain. Add to the mixture along with the lemon rind. Stir with a wooden spoon to mix and the mixture will go quite thick in the basin. Pour the filling into the chilled biscuit pie crust and spread level. Wash the strawberries and cut in half and peel and slice up the kiwi and then arrange them in a ring around the edge of the pie to decorate. Chill the pie until firm. Then cut in wedges and serve.

Lucia and Sam Hill
Lucia: I love chocolate and apples. In the kitchen I like baking puddings.
Sam: My favourite food is fish and chips. In the kitchen I help squeeze the lemons.

# mars bar mousse

● **3 mars bars** ● **1 tbsp milk** ● **300ml double cream, whipped**
**Decoration:**
● **maltesers** ● **4 tbsp double cream, whipped**

Place mars bars and milk in a microwave for 3 – 4 minutes

stirring half-way through.  Fold in the whipped cream.

Place in the fridge for 1 hour.  Put a blob of cream on the

top and decorate with maltesers before serving!

Georgia Stone

Some of my
favourite foods are
chips, oranges and
apples. I help with the
cooking especially
making pancakes.

# tiramisu allafrutta

- **400g mascarpone cheese** ● **2 x 15ml spoons caster sugar** ● **200g ready-to-serve custard, chilled** ● **500g ripe strawberries** ● **3 x 15ml spoons whipped cream** ● **10 amaretti biscuits, roughly crumbled** ● **200ml apple juice** ● **25 sponge fingers**

Place the mascarpone cheese in a bowl and soften with a fork. Add the sugar and custard and mix together well. Cut a quarter of the strawberries into very small pieces and fold gently into the mascarpone mixture with the whipped cream and a third of the biscuits. Slice the rest of the strawberries, leaving a few whole to decorate. Dip some of the sponge fingers into the apple juice and use to cover the bottom of a glass serving dish. Arrange a layer of the sliced strawberries on top and cover with a layer of mascarpone. Repeat with another layer of soaked biscuits, more strawberries and mascarpone cream. Continue until the dish is filled, with a final layer of mascarpone. Decorate with the remaining crumbled biscuits and the reserved strawberries. Chill for at least 5 hours, preferably overnight, before serving.
Serves: 6

Jacob Caunter

I like to eat pizza and apples. At home I sometimes help to make the food.

# quinn's recipe for baked chocolate cheesecake

- 175g digestive biscuits
- 75g butter
- 350g cream cheese
- 75g brown sugar
- 3 eggs
- 250ml soured cream
- 1 large bar chocolate

Crush the biscuits and stir in the melted butter. Press into a deep cake tin (20cm) loose bottomed lined with grease-proof paper. Keep refrigerated while preparing filling. For the filling put the cream cheese, sugar, egg yolks and soured cream into a basin and beat until smooth. Melt the chocolate in a bowl over hot water. Whip the egg whites until soft peaks form. Fold the chocolate and egg whites into the cream cheese mixture. Spread over the biscuit base. Bake it in the oven at 180°C/350°F/Gas Mark 4 for 40–50 minutes or until filling is set. Cool.

Quinn Jones

I like to eat cottage pie and apples. I make breakfast, lunch and sometimes tea!

# chocolate fudge pudding

- **2 tbsp melted margarine** ● **1 tsp vanilla essence**
- **1 cup self-raising flour** ● **½ tsp salt**
- **¾ cup sugar** ● **2 tbsp cocoa** ● **½ cup milk**

**Topping** ● **¾ cup sugar** ● **¼ cup cocoa** ● **1¾ cups hot water**

Mix all the dry ingredients together in a bowl. Then add the vanilla essence, melted margarine and mix together with the milk until stiff. Put into a large buttered pie dish. Then mix ¼ cup cocoa with ¾ cup of sugar (brown is best) and sprinkle on top of mixture in pie dish. Carefully pour on 1¾ cups of hot water. Bake in a moderately hot oven for about 1¼ hours.

Amy Bath

I love tomato soup. At home I get things ready for egg on toast.

# chocolate mousse

- 125g plain chocolate broken into pieces
- 4 large eggs
- 50g white chocolate

Put the plain chocolate in the heatproof dish. Place the bowl on a pan of simmering water (5cm deep) and allow the chocolate to melt. Separate the eggs. Pour the egg whites into a mixing bowl and put the yolks into a small bowl. Remove the melted chocolate from the heat and stir well. Cool a little. Beat the yolks and slowly add them to the chocolate, stirring well. Whisk the egg whites in the mixing bowl until they are firm and will stand up in soft peaks. With the spatula gently fold the whites into the chocolate and egg yolk mixture until evenly mixed. Carefully pour the mousse into four serving dishes and leave to set in the fridge for 2 hours. Decorate with grated white chocolate.

Oliver Thomasson

I love HOT chicken curry! And apple crumble. In the kitchen I like baking cakes and bread.

# flake cheesecake

- 125g butter ● 225g digestive biscuits
● 350g cream cheese ● 75g caster sugar ● 100g cadburys
bournville chocolate ● 125ml milk ● 20ml gelatine
● 2 large oranges ● 3 eggs ● 284ml double cream, lightly
whipped ● 6 chocolate flakes

Melt the butter, stir in the finely crushed biscuits then press half the mixture into a lined 20cm loose bottomed cake tin. Chill. Cream the cheese and sugar together. Melt the chocolate in the milk then cool slightly before mixing into the cheese mixture with the gelatine dissolved in 2 tbsp of boiling water. Finely grate the rind of 1 orange then segment both, reserve 8 segments and chop the remainder. Fold the orange rind and chopped pieces into the mixture with half the lightly whipped cream. Pour into the tin and leave to set. When set, carefully press the remaining biscuit mixture onto the cheesecake and chill. Gently turn cheesecake out onto a plate. Spread the top with remaining whipped cream. Decorate edge with thin pieces of flake and orange segments in the centre.

Joe Landricombe

I love to eat chips – I like bananas as well. Sometimes I help cook tea.

# bon appetit!

# la garbure bearnaise

- 4 – 5 large potatoes
- 4 carrots
- 2 large leeks
- 1 large turnip
- 4 slices bacon
- 1 onion with 1 clove
- 3 sprigs parsley
- 1 sprig thyme
- 1 clove garlic
- bouquet garni
- salt and pepper

Cut bacon into small chunks and fry in a large casserole pan with a little oil. Cut all vegetables into small chunks, except onion and garlic. When bacon is cooked, add all vegetables. Add the peeled garlic, bouquet garni and the onion. Pour cold water in the pan until ¾ full and add salt and pepper. For a better taste, add marrowbone from beef veal. Cook for at least 1 hour.

Serves: 2

Cook 1-2 days in advance as the soup tastes better when reheated.

Tomas Nicholas

I like to eat chicken korma and I like melon. At home I help make the tea.

# lamb chops in papillote

- **4 loin chops** ● **2½ boiled eggs** ● **40g fresh breadcrumbs**
- **small clove of garlic** ● **½ tsp salt** ● **pinch of pepper**
- **1 tbsp chopped parsley** ● **40g melted butter**

Chop hard boiled eggs finely and mix with breadcrumbs.

Chop parsley and garlic and melt the butter. Coat each

chop with the above and wrap in a piece of foil and bake in

a hot oven (200-220°C) for 30 minutes. When cooked open

foil, put into a grill pan and grill until golden brown.

Serves: 4

note
Pronounced 'pap-er-lot-e', this is a traditional recipe from
New Zealand

Harrison Harvey

I like to eat pizza
and raspberries.
mummy does
the cooking and
washing up.

# bobotie

- 1kg minced beef or mutton ● 1 slice white bread ● 1 medium onion, finely chopped ● 125ml seedless raisins ● 125ml blanched almonds ● 15ml apricot jam ● 15ml fruit chutney ● 25ml lemon juice ● 5ml chopped mixed herbs ● 10ml curry powder ● 5ml turmeric ● 10ml salt ● 10ml oil ● 3 eggs ● 4 bay or lemon leaves

Soak bread in 125ml milk, squeeze, dry and mix with minced beef or mutton. Mix in all other ingredients except for remaining milk, oil, eggs, bay or lemon leaves. Heat oil in a frying pan and brown meat mixture lightly. Turn out into a casserole. Beat eggs with remaining milk and pour over meat. Garnish with bay or lemon leaves and bake at 180°C/ 350°F/Gas Mark 4 for 50 minutes.

Serves: 8
This is a South African recipe

Callum Lloyd
I really like Cornish pasties and watermelon. In the kitchen I help by washing and chopping the mushrooms.

# cloutie dumpling

- ½ pint water
- ¾ cup white sugar
- 2 eggs, beaten
- ½ lb plain flour
- 1 rounded tsp mixed spice
- 1 rounded tsp cinnamon
- 1 tsp bicarbonate of soda
- ½ lb margarine
- ½ lb mixed fruit
- ½ lb sultanas
- 1 tbsp treacle

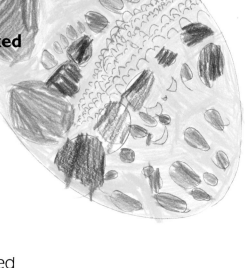

Put the water, mixed spice, cinnamon, fruit, margarine and treacle into a saucepan on the cooker. Bring to the boil and simmer for one minute. Remove from heat and mix in the sieved flour and bicarbonate of soda. Add egg. Pour into medium sized microwave suitable bowl which has been lined with enough cling film to go well over the sides, but do not cover the mixture with cling film. Microwave for 9 minutes (650 watt microwave) 7½ minutes (900 watt microwave).

note
This is a Scottish recipe

Ryan McGill

I like carrots and broccoli. Me and my mummy make cakes.

# ground beef and noodle casserole

● **225g egg noodles** ● **30ml oil** ● **450g ground beef** ● **I clove garlic, finely chopped** ● **2 beef bouillon cubes** ● **450ml boiling water** ● **I25ml tomato** ● **¼ tsp dried mixed herbs** ● **60ml cornstarch** ● **salt, pepper, sugar to taste** ● **300ml sharp cheddar cheese** ● **½ tsp paprika pepper**

Cook the noodles in boiling salted water until tender but not soft then drain and rinse.  Heat the oil in a large skillet, brown the ground beef and add the garlic. Stir frequently during the cooking.  Dissolve the beef bouillon cubes in the hot water and add to the browned meat. Add the tomato and herbs, cover and simmer for 15 minutes. Thicken with the cornstarch blended with a little cold water.  Taste and season carefully.  Put half the cooked noodles in an oven proof dish.  Cover with half the meat, then half the cheese. Repeat the layers with the remaining ingredients. Sprinkle the top layer of cheese with paprika pepper.  Cover tightly. Bake at 350°F/180°C/Gas Mark 4 for 1 hour 15 minutes.

Serves: 4-6
note
Serve with a green salad or a cooked green vegetable.

This is a Canadian family recipe

James Frost

I love to eat chocolate and tomatoes. At home mum cooks the dinners – when daddy cooks it all goes wrong!

# australian quiche

- **3-4 eggs, beaten** ● **225g bacon, diced**
- **225g cheese, grated** ● **I medium size onion, chopped**
- **2 large mushrooms** ● **½ small sweetcorn**
- **I pepper** ● **pepper and salt**

Mix eggs, bacon, cheese and onion together in a
mixing bowl.  Add mushrooms, sweet corn, salt and
pepper to suit your taste.  Grease a quiche dish and
pour in the mixture.  Add sliced tomato to the top.
Bake at 180°C/350°F/Gas Mark 4 for approximately
40 minutes.

Katie & Phoebe Sherrel

I like eating fajitas
and cheese crackers.
Mum cooks the food,
dad does the drinks
and me and my
sister lay the table.

# korean kebabs

- **400g chicken fillets, roughly chopped**
- **2 tbsp peanut butter** ● **2 tbsp soy sauce**
- **1 tbsp olive oil** ● **1 tbsp spring onions, roughly chopped** ● **1 clove garlic, roughly chopped**
- **1 tsp sesame seeds**

Place all ingredients, except chicken, into a bowl and mix thoroughly. Add chicken to mixture, cover and place in the fridge to marinate for a couple of hours. When ready to cook (barbeque), thread chicken onto skewers and place on barbeque, turning as required. Use any spare marinade to baste.

Serves: 4

note
Serve with green salad or new potatoes.

Henry Warrender

Some of my favourite foods are chocolate and raspberries. At home I sometimes make hot drinks.

# kottbullar (swedish meatballs)

- ½ cup fresh breadcrumbs ● I cup milk ● I onion, chopped
- 300g butter ● 300g ground beef ● 100g ground pork
- I egg ● salt and white pepper ● all spice (optional)

Soak breadcrumbs in milk.  Brown the onion in butter.
Mix meat, bread mixture, onion and egg and season
with salt and pepper (all spice if Christmas).  Mix lightly
adding a little water if needed.  Make a meatball (small
ball made with a wet hand).  Fry in a little oil, make
more meatballs and fry.  Place meatballs on a rinsed
plate.  When frying meatballs in oil and butter, do not
fry too many at once and shake pan frequently so
they stay round.  Place cooked meatballs on a warmed
serving dish.

Serves: 4

Eleanor Stone

I love eating pasta
bake and oranges. I
set the table and do
the dishes.

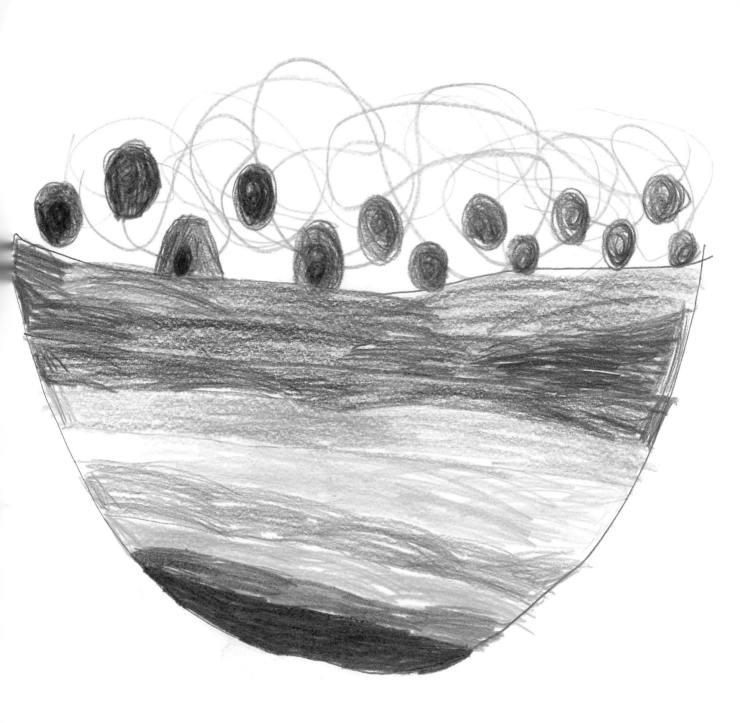

# kartofel puffer (potato pancakes)

- 3 – 4 large potatoes
- 2 eggs
- 1 large onion
- 1 tbsp oats
- pinch of salt

Grate the potatoes and onion into a bowl.  Add the eggs and oats and mix together.  Spoon out burger-sized portions into a frying pan.  Fry both sides until golden brown and serve.

Serves: 4

note
This recipe was given to me by my German Nan and can be served as a chip or potato substitute.

Cara Welsh

I like peas and strawberries. I help cook the dinner.

# cirniky (a russian recipe)

- **2½ tbsp sugar** ● **½ cup flour**
- **300g cottage cheese (natural)** ● **sunflower oil** ● **I egg**

Put the cottage cheese into a bowl and mix well
with the sugar, egg and flour.  Roll the mixture into a
ball and squash the ball into a circle.  Fry with oil until
golden on both sides.

Serves: 4

note
Serve with Greek yogurt, jam, honey or condensed milk.

Daria & Marta Yushchenko

Daria: I love roast
chicken and fruit
salad. At home I unload
the dishwasher.

# thai green seafood with noodles

● **1 onion chopped** ● **1-2 garlic cloves chopped** ● **½ cube of coconut milk in ½ pint of boiling water** ● **juice of ½ lemon** ● **1 chilli, finely chopped** ● **½ pint of fish stock** ● **2 stalks of lemongrass or equivalent** ● **bunch of coriander chopped** ● **seafood mix (prawns, squid mussels, fish)** ● **noodles**

Fry onion and garlic.  Boil water for noodles.  Add coconut milk mixture, lemon juice, chilli, lemongrass, fish stock and coriander to the onion and garlic. Stir and simmer.  Now add the seafood, simmer until cooked through.  Serve on a bed of noodles by itself or with a sweet pea and tomato salad as well.

Serves: 4

We love this meal as it's quick and easy to prepare and tastes great and guests always love it.

Blue Ewer

My favourite meal is a cooked breakfast.

# vegetarian german pasta salad

● **250g dried macaroni or pasta shells** ● **10 vegetarian hot dog sausages, chopped into bite size pieces** ● **280g cooked peas** ● **5 pickled gherkins, drained and chopped** ● **2 hard boiled eggs, shelled and roughly chopped** ● **½ onion, finely chopped** ● **4 tbsp mayonnaise** ● **2 tbsp wine vinegar** ● **1 tsp german mustard** ● **salt and pepper** ● **hard boiled eggs to garnish**

Cook the macaroni according to the packet instructions.

Once cooked refresh the pasta under cold water to prevent overcooking. Drain and leave to cool. When pasta is cold add the remaining ingredients mixing them well in a large bowl, season with salt and pepper, cover and leave in the fridge to chill. Serve with hard boiled egg wedges.

Melissa & Ben Beaumont

I like pizza, broccoli and carrots. Mum clears away the dishes when we finish eating.

# reibekucher (german potato pancakes)

- 450g potatoes (not new) ● 50g plain flour
- I egg ● pinch salt ● sunflower oil for frying

Peel and grate the potatoes as finely as you can until they are a pulp. Stir in the flour, salt and egg. Mix well. Heat a shallow puddle of sunflower oil in a non-stick frying pan until very hot. Pour in a ladleful of mixture and flatten slightly. If you have a big pan you can fry 2 or 3 at the same time. Fry for 3 – 4 minutes on each side until golden.
Serves: Makes 5 – 6 pancakes

note

Can be eaten plain with a soup or stew, or sweet with golden syrup or jam topping. We like ham best for savoury things and golden syrup for sweet things.

Emily Tutty

I like pizza and noodles. I help at home by getting my own breakfast.

# south seas christmas pudding

**Pudding:** ● **225g can pineapple** ● **100g caster sugar** ● **I orange, grated rind only** ● **2 eggs, beaten** ● **75g self-raising flour, sifted** ● **50g fresh breadcrumbs** ● **50g glace cherries, quartered** ● **25g angelica** ● **I tbsp golden syrup**  *Harry & chestnut*
**Tangy butter:** ● **50g butter** ● **50g caster sugar** ● **2 eggs, beaten** ● **I orange, juice only** ● **juice from pineapple (in pudding)** ● **I tsp cornflour**

For the pudding, drain pineapple, reserving juice, cut 3 half-rings and put aside, chop remainder coarsely.  Cream margarine and sugar, add orange rind and beat in eggs. Fold in flour and breadcrumbs.  Add chopped pineapple, raisins, cherries, angelica and mix well.  Butter a 1 litre basin, place syrup in bottom and arrange pineapple rings in a circle.  Spoon sponge mixture on top and level it.  Cover with buttered paper and foil.  Place basin in saucepan of boiling water so water comes  two thirds up sides of basin and boil for 1¾ hours.  To make the tangy butter, place a double saucepan or basin over boiling water and melt butter.  Add sugar, beaten eggs and fruit juice made up to 300ml with water.  Cook together until hot, stirring occasionally.  Blend cornflour with a little water and add, stirring until thick.  Serve hot.

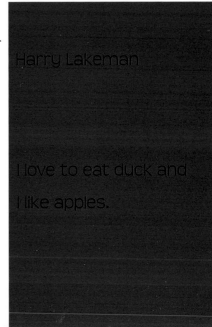

Harry Lakeman

I love to eat duck and I like apples.

# anzac biscuits

- **100g butter** ● **1 tbsp golden syrup** ● **1 tsp baking soda**
- **2 tbsp boiling water** ● **1 cup sugar** ● **1 cup coconut**
- **1 cup rolled oats** ● **¾ cup flour**

Melt butter with the golden syrup in a mixing bowl. Dissolve the baking soda in the boiling water and add to the bowl. Add the sugar, coconut, rolled oats and flour and mix thoroughly. Take small teaspoons of mixture and place on a cold, greased oven sheet. Allow space and cook for 30 minutes at 150°C/300°F/Gas Mark 2.

note
Anzac stands for Australian and New Zealand Army Corps

Maia Hay-Newnham

My favourite food is a roast, I also like grapes. I help out by loading and unloading the dishwasher.

# american pancakes with maple syrup

- rapeseed oil ● 100g self-raising flour
- 1 egg ● 150ml milk ● butter
- maple syrup or maple flavoured golden syrup

Whisk the flour, milk, egg and salt together so there are no lumps. Coat a well seasoned cast iron frying pan with a little oil and heat. If the pan starts to smoke back off the heat a little. Using a table spoon place a spoonful of the mix into the pan and cook for about a minute, turn and cook other side for about 30 seconds. The pancakes should be golden brown with tubular bubbles running from top to bottom. Try and cook about four at a time and once cooked keep warm. Serve with butter melted over the top and maple syrup poured over.

Note that rapeseed oil is very neutral in flavour. Olive oil or sunflower oil for example could taint the pancakes.

Seb Musgrave

Some of my favourite foods are prawns and strawberries. In the kitchen we make lots of cakes and strawberry pies.

# pepernoten (ginger nuts)

- 200g self-raising flour ● pinch of salt
- 150g dutch syrup (stroop) ● 2 tsp cinnamon powder ● 1 tsp ground coriander ● 1 tsp ground nutmeg ● ½ tsp ginger powder
- pinch of ground anise seed

Preheat the oven to 160°C/325°F/Gas Mark 3. Sift the flour with salt and spices into a bowl. Make a hollow in the top of the mound and pour in the syrup. Mix everything from the centre and knead into thick dough. Place in the fridge for 1 hour. Roll out the dough to a thickness of about ½ cm and make into small marble-sized balls, for example by using an apple corer. Place the marbles on grease proof paper. Press them down slightly. Put in the centre of the preheated oven and bake for 15-20 minutes until done and golden brown.

These are traditionally eaten when the Dutch celebrate "Sinterklaas" (St Nicholas) on the 5th December.

Amie Gregory

I love eating pizzas and cherries. I help in the kitchen by cutting up some of the vegetables.

# swedish chocolate balls

- **100g butter** ● **150g icing sugar** ● **1 tbsp cocoa**
● **6 tbsp porridge oats** ● **3 tbsp coffee granules (put the coffee in a mug and then pour in 3-4tsp of boiling water and stir)** ● **desiccated coconut**

Whisk butter and sugar together until smooth.  Pour in cocoa, oats and coffee and stir until all mixed together.

Put your dough into a bowl and cool in the fridge for about 20-25 minutes.  Take a piece of dough and roll into a small ball, do the same for the rest of the dough and then roll each ball in coconut.  Keep them cool in the fridge.

Serves: Makes about 30 balls

Sophia Parr

I love pizza and any fruit. I enjoy baking at home.

# bana brith (welsh bread)

- **450g mixed fruit** • **2 cups soft brown sugar**
- **2 cups self-raising flour** • **1 egg, beaten** • **1 tbsp sherry**
- **1 cup cold strained tea, without milk**

Place fruit, sugar and tea in a basin and leave to
soak overnight. The next day, stir in sherry, egg
and flour and turn mixture into a well greased tin.
Bake at 150°C/300°F/Gas Mark 3 for 2 hours.

Jordan Stidson

My favourite food is
duck and I like apples. I
help wash the dishes.

# american muffins

● **1½ cups of plain flour** ● **½ cup sugar** ● **2 tsp baking powder**
● **1 egg** ● **½ cup milk** ● **¼ cup vegetable oil**
**Flavouring options:** ● **1 cup chopped apple and ½ teaspoon**
**cinnamon** ● **1oz / 25 g chocolate chips** ● **¼ cup raisins**
● **½ carton blueberry yogurt**

Sieve together the flour, sugar, salt and baking

powder.  Stir in the flavouring of your choice.

Beat the egg, add milk and oil.  Stir into the dry

ingredients until evenly mixed.  Fill muffin tins lined

with cake cases.  Bake in the oven at 200°C for 20

– 25 minutes.  Cool on a wire rack.

Serves: Makes approximately 10 delicious American

muffins

This is a recipe for hungry hordes – accuracy is not

important.

Matt Watts

My favourite food is

fudge! I like carrots.

In the kitchen...I do

nothing...except cook

custard!

American

Muffins

# babcia's migola towa babka (granny's almond cake)

- 200g sugar ● 150g margarine ● 200g self-raising flour
- 50g ground almonds ● 5 eggs ● 1 lemon (juice from)
- 1tsp baking powder ● vanilla essence ● orange peel from 1 orange ● almond essence

Mix margarine and sugar and beat until smooth.

Add egg yolks, flour and flavourings. Beat egg whites to foam and fold into the cake mixture.

Bake at 180°C/350°F/Gas Mark 4 for approximately 1 hour. When cool, sprinkle icing sugar on the top.

Use continental fluted baking mould for pretty effect

Alex Howard-Harwood

I like jacket potatoes with cheese and strawberries. Once I cooked mine and mummy and daddy's tea!

# pinaattiohukaiset (spinach pancakes)

- **400 ml of milk at room temperature** ● **I egg** ● **I tsp salt**
- **250 ml plain flour** ● **I tbsp oil** ● **200 g frozen spinach**
  **– squeezed dry and chopped** ● **oil for frying**

Mix the ingredients together in the given order using an electric mixer. If possible, leave the batter to rest for up to 30 mins before making the pancakes. Cook the pancakes on each side until they have browned slightly. Keep them warm. Serve the spinach pancakes as a vegetable course - accompanied, if you like, by lingonberries.

Mustikka Piiras

Enon Koulu School, Finland

This is one of the favourites of the children from our link school in Finland.

# korvapuustit (cinnamon buns)

**Dough:** ● 500 ml milk ● 50g yeast (one packet)
● 150-200 ml sugar ● 1 tsp salt ● 2 tsp ground cardamom
● 1 egg ● 150-200 g margarine or butter ● 1 kg flour
**Filling:** ● melted butter ● cinnamon ● sugar
**Topping:** ● 1 egg ● coarse sugar

Dissolve yeast into lukewarm milk in a mixing bowl.
Add sugar, salt, cardamom and egg and mix. Add half
of the flour and stir into a soft dough. Mix butter
into the dough and add more flour as needed. The
dough is ready when it is no longer sticky. Cover the
mixing bowl with a tea towel and leave to rise in a
warm place for approximately 30 minutes. Pour the
dough onto a floured surface, knead and then halve
the dough. Roll out one part into a rectangular sheet
(approximately 1 cm thick) with a rolling pin. Spread
melted butter onto the sheet and then sprinkle
plenty of sugar and cinnamon on top of it.

Roll the sheet up tightly, starting from the longer side. Cut the bar into even, triangular pieces. Turn the pieces upwards and press down the centres of the buns with your finger, so that the cut edges bulge out on both sides. Repeat the process with the other half of the dough. Place the buns onto baking trays covered with greaseproof paper and prove for 30 minutes. Afterwards brush the buns with beaten egg and sprinkle with coarse sugar. Bake at 225°C on the middle rack of the oven for approximately 10–15 minutes, until golden brown.

Enon Koulu School, Finland

Another recipe from our Finnish friends!

# pack a picnic

# mini burger bites

● **400g pork or turkey mince** ● **I egg** ● **I tbsp crunchy peanut butter** ● **salt & pepper** ● **I tbsp sweet chilli dipping sauce (optional)** ● **4 slices bread made into breadcrumbs** ● **2 tbsp oil**

Mix all ingredients apart from oil together in a bowl. Heat the oil in a frying pan and shallow fry small balls of the mixture flattened (about the size of a 50p piece). If using chilli sauce cook on a really low heat as the sugar in the sauce makes them burn easily.

Serve with green salad or crusty bread.

Sam Clifton

I like to eat salad! When I help to make cakes sometimes I lick out the bowl.

# pooh sticks

● **325g plain flour** ● **150g cheddar cheese, finely grated** ● **2 eggs, beaten** ● **150g butter or margarine, cut into pieces** ● **salt and freshly ground black pepper**

Preheat oven to 200°C/Gas Mark 6. Lightly brush 2 baking sheets with oil. Put the flour and a little seasoning into a bowl, add the butter and rub into the flour until it resembles fine breadcrumbs. Stir in 100g of the grated cheese. Reserve about a tablespoon of the egg and add the rest into the flour and cheese and mix to a smooth dough. Knead mixture on a floured surface, roll out to about 5mm thick and cut into 10cm long sticks and place on the baking sheets. Brush sticks with the reserved egg and sprinkle with the remaining cheese. Cook for approx 10 minutes until golden brown.

Serve in party paper cups.

Jessica Leach

I love spaghetti bolognese and I like carrots. I help mummy with the cooking.

# benjamin's brunch

- **2 slices granary bread** • **tuna mayonnaise mixture** • **lettuce**
- **cucumber (4 x slices) finely sliced** • **2 cherry tomatoes sliced**
- **grated carrot**

Toast the bread and cut out shapes using a fish cutter. Spread the tuna mayonnaise over the fish shapes. Arrange lettuce as seaweed on a plate and make coral shape patterns with the cucumber, tomato and carrot. Place fish shapes over the sea scene and enjoy!

Benjamin Lock

My favourite food is fish.

# golden crispy chicken fingers

● **2 chicken breasts** ● **I egg** ● **I tbsp milk** ● **50g cornflakes** ● **oil**

Cut the chicken breast into strips. Beat an egg and milk together in a shallow dish. Crush cornflakes with a rolling pin and spread on a plate. Dip the chicken strips in the egg mixture and coat with the cornflakes. Gently shallow fry in sunflower oil until golden brown and cooked through.

note

Before cooking freeze any extras on a tray and then store in a freezer bag.

Alex Parr

I love to eat spaghetti bolognese.

# salmon and cream cheese croissants

- **1 tin croissant dough** ● **2 skinless, boneless salmon fillets**
- **cream cheese** ● **1 vegetable stock cube** ● **chopped chives**

Preheat oven to 180°C/350°F/Gas Mark 4. Dissolve the stock cube in a saucepan of boiling water and poach the salmon for 10 – 12 minutes. Drain and flake salmon. Open out croissant dough and spread each triangle with cream cheese and chopped chives. Place a generous tablespoonful of salmon at the wide part of each triangle and then roll up to form a croissant. Place on a greased baking sheet or pizza stone and bake for 15 minutes until dough is golden.

note
These can also be made with smoked salmon if preferred. Delicious hot or cold.

Jonathan White

I like cheese and petits pois. I sometimes help make bread and I wash and dry up..and lay the table!

# ben's cheesy sage scones

- **227g plain flour** ● **1tsp** ● **salt** ● **1 tsp bicarbonate of soda** ● **1tbsp freshly chopped sage**
- **pinch of paprika** ● **2tsp mixed wholegrain mustard**
- **150ml skimmed milk** ● **30g demerara sugar**
- **60g butter** ● **85g strong mature cheddar, grated**

Grease a baking tray. Cut butter into small pieces, add to sifted flour, bicarbonate of soda and salt. Rub in fat until mixture looks like fine breadcrumbs then add grated cheese, sage and paprika. Stir in sugar and mustard, then gradually add milk, stirring with a thin wooden spoon to make a soft dough. Collect mixture together and knead lightly on a floured surface. Cut into circles with a cutter and brush the tops with a little milk. Bake in the top of the oven for 12-15 mins at 220 c.

Serves: Makes 12 scones

Benjamin Foster, artwork by Jack Pritchard

Benjamin: I love chicken. I help mummy make cheese straws.

Jack: I love pesto and I look after the pasta while it's cooking.

# cheesy shapes

- **50g self-raising flour**
- **100g grated cheddar cheese**
- **pinch salt**
- **50g butter or margarine**
- **small amount grated parmesan (optional)**

Preheat oven to 190°C (fan 170°C)/Gas Mark 5.

Combine all ingredients with your fingers, rubbing them together till crumbly and then form a ball.

Roll the ball of dough on a floured surface until it is 3-4mm thick. Use fun shaped cutters to cut the biscuits out and place them on a greased and floured baking tray. Bake for 10-12 minutes in the oven.

Enjoy when warm or cold.

Sam Tutty

I really like carrots.

# chicken drumsticks with lemon and honey

- **8 chicken drumsticks**
- **3 tbsp runny honey**
- **1 tbsp light soy sauce**
- **juice of 1 lemon**

Heat oven to 175°C. Mix the honey, lemon juice and soy sauce in a shallow ovenproof dish. Add the chicken and coat with the sauce. Marinade for 30 minutes. Coat the chicken again and put in the oven for 45 minutes. Check the chicken is cooked and leave to cool. Wrap foil around the ends of the drumsticks to serve. YUM YUM.

Serves: 4

Christian Poole

I like noodles and mango and I enjoy baking!

# pinwheels

- 1 packet puff pastry
- 400g of mature cheddar cheese
- 1 onion
- 10 rashers of unsmoked back bacon
- pepper
- 1 egg

Start by grating the cheese, dicing the onion, and chopping the bacon removing any fat and rind. On a lightly floured surface roll out the pastry to a large square shape. Cover the pastry with the grated cheese leaving approximately 1cm around the edge, then the onion and the bacon, season with pepper to taste. Lightly beat the egg, and brush along the edge furthest from you. From the edge nearest you start to roll the pastry (like a Swiss roll) fairly tightly, don't worry if some filling falls out it can be put in after. Make sure you stick down the edge with the egg on it and give it all a good squeeze. Using a sharp knife cut it into rounds and place on lined baking trays. With the rest of the egg glaze the top of them lightly and add some more cheese if you want. Bake in the oven on 200°C/400°C/Gas Mark 6 for 20-30mins.

note
This recipe can be modified to taste. As a general rule you can get 24 pinwheels from 1 packet of pastry.

Megan Gomm

I like fish and chips and apples. My mum cooks the dinner and one day I helped.

# joe's sporty energy bars

- 140g dark or milk chocolate broken into pieces
- 140g milk chocolate 110g pecan nuts (or alternative) 110g ready to eat apricots
- 140g organic porridge oats 25g rice crispies 75g raisins 1 tbsp molasses syrup 145ml whole condensed milk
- baking tin, 10" x 6"

Preheat oven to 180°C/350°F/Gas Mark 4. Toast pecan nuts for 7 minutes and chop roughly. Chop apricots to same size as pecans, then in a large bowl mix oats, rice crispies, bran flakes, apricots, pecans and raisins. In a small saucepan heat molasses and condensed milk until warm and thoroughly blended then pour into bowl. Mix well with wooden spoon. Simply tip mixture into baking tin, press down evenly. Leave until cold. Melt chocolate in different bowls. When cereal mixture is cool tip out upside down onto a board. Using a tablespoon put spoonfuls of dark or milk chocolate over top of cereal cake leaving spaces in between. Do the same with the white chocolate but this time fill up the gaps. Using a palette knife, mix two chocolates together making a swirling pattern. Chill in fridge for one hour. Enjoy!

Joe Lloyd

I love rice with prawns and strawberries. My mum cooks and so does my dad.

# chocolate fudge

- **400g granulated sugar**
- **25g butter**
- **250ml condensed milk (unsweetened)**
- **125g plain chocolate**
- **2 tbsp water**
- **1 tsp vanilla essence**

Put all the ingredients, except the vanilla essence in a pan (you will need a large one).  Stand the pan on a low heat until the sugar has melted then turn up the heat and boil fairly rapidly for 25 – 30 minutes.  Do not forget to stir occasionally in case the sugar is sticking to the bottom of the pan.  Then, take the pan off the heat, stir in the vanilla essence and beat the mixture with a wooden spoon until it thickens and looks creamy.  Turn it out as quickly as possible onto a greased tin.  When it is almost cold, cut the fudge into pieces with a sharp knife – be very careful when you use this.  When the fudge is quite cold, turn it out of the tin onto a piece of greaseproof paper.  After a short time, pack it away into a tin – if you haven't eaten it all by then!

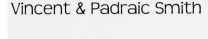

Vincent & Padraic Smith

Padraic: I like pizza with anchovies and salad.

Vincent: My favourite foods are roast duck and sweetcorn.

# nan's gooseberry patties

**Pastry:** ● 200g of flour - self raising or plain ● 50g of margarine
● **50g of lard** ● **cold water to mix**
**Filling:** ● **gooseberries, approximately 200g** ● **caster sugar** ● **milk**
**To serve:** ● **caster sugar** ● **clotted cream**

Rub fats into flour until it is like fine breadcrumbs. Mix with cold water to make a smooth dough. Wrap in cling film and chill in fridge for 30 minutes. Lightly dust a surface with flour. Halve the pastry mix and roll out one half to approximately 5mm thick. Cut out rounds, slightly larger than the bun tin to be used. Roll out the other half and cut out rounds the same size as the bun tin as lids for your gooseberry patties. Repeat until pastry ball is used up. Line bun tins with pastry bases and place 4 or 5 gooseberries in each case. Add half a teaspoon of sugar, damp the edges and place tops on bases sealing edges firmly. With a skewer make a hole in the lid. Brush with milk and bake for 15 to 20 minutes until they are golden brown at 200°C or Gas Mark 6. Turn out onto a wire rack. Serve with sugar and cream.

Serves: Makes 12 patties

Anna Hudson with artwork by Lauren Davis

I enjoy summer fruit pudding and fruit salad with grapes and kiwi fruit. In the kitchen I love baking gingerbread men.

# toffee apples

- 10 red apples ● 250g butter ● 1 cup sugar
- 3 tbsp water ● ¼ tsp salt
- 1 tsp vanilla ● wooden skewers

Remove stalks from apples and push a wooden skewer into each one. Place toffee ingredients in saucepan and heat until sugar dissolves, stirring occasionally. Bring to boil. Boil rapidly, without stirring, until the toffee reaches 145°C (280°F) or until a spoonful of mixture, when dropped in cold water, separates into threads which are hard but not brittle. Carefully dip apples into toffee, one at a time. Cover apple completely. Plunge into ice water for 5 seconds. Stand on well-oiled greaseproof (waxed) paper until set.

Harrison Stone

I love all kinds of pasta and mackerel... that I've caught myself! In the kitchen I like baking cookies (just for me!).

# scottish tablets (fudge)

**900g granulated sugar** ● **1 tin condensed milk** ● **1 teacup of milk** ● **100g butter**

Place all the ingredients in a large pan and bring slowly to the boil. Boil steadily for 20 minutes. Remove from heat and beat for 5 minutes, then pour into greased roasting tin. After about 15 minutes mark into squares with a knife.

Leave for 24 hours before eating (if possible!!).

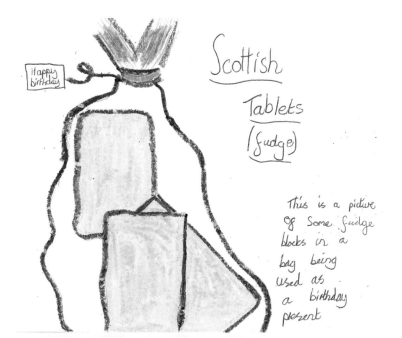

Scottish Tablets (fudge)

This is a picture of some fudge blocks in a bag being used as a birthday present

George Warrender

I love any fruit crumble and oranges. In the kitchen I burn food! Especially roast chicken!

# date balls

- **500g chopped dates** • **250g butter**
- **250g sugar** • **1 whisked egg** • **1 packet of digestive biscuits, crumbled** • **1 packet coconut**

Melt the butter and sugar over a low heat in a saucepan.  Add dates and stir thoroughly.  Add some of the dates to the whisked egg and then add the mixture to the saucepan, stirring all the time.  Remove from the heat and add the crumbled digestive biscuits.  Roll the mixture into balls, big or small, and then roll them in the coconut.  Freeze for a night.

Mariza Celliers

# bumble's homemade lemonade

- **3 large lemons** **700g granulated sugar**
- **25g vitamin C powder (available from health food shops)**

Thinly slice lemons and place in a large bowl. Add
sugar and vitamin C powder. Pour on 2.25 litres
boiling water and stir well to dissolve sugar. Cover
and leave for 24 hours. Strain and store in a cool
place. Use as cordial, dilute to taste.

Alex Milham

I like fishfingers. In the
kitchen I help mummy
stir things.

# sam's summer shakes

**300g kitley strawberries** **250ml whole milk** **4 scoops devon ice cream – 2 x vanilla and 2 x strawberry** **icing sugar to taste – if necessary** **8 ice cubes – crushed in a bag with a rolling pin at the last minute**

Mix the strawberries and milk together using a hand blender. Add ice-cream and blend again (add icing sugar if required). Pour into glasses. Add crushed ice and a straw to each serving.

Serves: 4

Substitute ice cream with fromage frais and pour into freezer moulds for scrumptious creamy ice lollies. Try different fruits for endless flavours, peach and raspberry, strawberry and pear or blueberry and apple (stew and chill apples first).

Sam Gingell

I love yorkshire pudding. At home I help make pancakes.

# breakfast power smoothie

- **20g porridge oats** • **I ripe banana** • **2 tsp honey**
- **I heaped tbsp greek yogurt** • **300ml milk**
- **8 ice cubes** • **mixed sunflower and pumpkin seeds**

Put all your ingredients into a

blender or food processor and

whiz until smooth.  Sprinkle with

seeds and serve with a straw.

Purple power! Add a handful of blueberries to make it
extra good for you and a very cool colour.

William Fay

My favourite food is
pasta and I like apples.
I help my mum make
cakes.

# hot mint choc chip drink

- **600ml milk**
- **142ml pot double cream**
- **100g chopped mint chocolate**

Pour the milk, double cream and chopped chocolate in a pan. Bring gently to the boil, whisking until smooth. Serve in individual cups or mugs, topped with mini marshmallows and a little grated chocolate.

Jonathan Pollard

I enjoy eating chicken pies and apples. I help make flapjacks.

barmy
baking

# golden harvest cake

● 175g margarine ● 175g caster sugar ● grated rind of 1 medium orange ● 3 medium eggs ● 225g self-raising flour ● 2 tbsp orange juice ● 175g sultanas ● 25g chopped walnuts

Cream together the margarine, sugar and orange rind until fluffy. Beat the eggs in a separate bowl until fluffy. Add the eggs to the mixture a little at a time beating well each time. With the last bit of egg add a small amount of flour. Fold in the flour, orange juice, walnuts and sultanas. Line a 7½ inch round baking tin and grease well. Add the mixture to the tin and bake in the middle of a pre-heated oven 160°C/325°F/Gas Mark 3. Cook for 1¼ hours and when cooked leave in the tin for 2–3 minutes. Take out of tin and place on a wire tray to cool.

Claire Brown

I like to eat spaghetti and I like strawberries and cherries. I normally help mummy grate the cheese.

# mud pie

- **175g butter** ● **1 tbsp cocoa powder** ● **125g caster sugar**
- **125g mixed dried fruit** ● **250g broken biscuits**
- **1 chocolate bar for topping** ● **chocolate strands**

Melt the butter and add the cocoa, sugar, fruit and biscuits. Mix together well. Place foil in a tin and pour in the mixture. Press down and place in the fridge. For the topping, melt the chocolate and spread on top of the pie. Decorate with chocolate strands.

Rachel Corrigan

I love chocolate sponge and roast chicken. At home mummy usually does the cooking.

# hocolate orange cake

- 1 large thin-skinned orange ● 6 eggs
- 1 heaped tsp baking powder
- ½ tsp bicarbonate of soda ● 200g ground almonds ● 250g caster sugar ● 50g cocoa

Put orange in a pan with cold water, bring to the boil and simmer gently for 2 hours. Drain, cool and cut the orange in half, removing pips. Pulp pith, peel and all in a food processor, or chop up into small chunks and use the hand blender. Once the fruit is cold, pre-heat the oven to 180°C/350°F/Gas Mark 4. Butter and line a 20cm spring form tin. Add the eggs, baking powder, bicarbonate of soda, almonds, sugar and cocoa to the orange in the food processor or electric hand blender. Blend ingredients. Pour into the cake tin and bake for an hour, checking after 45 minutes as you may have to cover with foil to prevent the cake from burning before it is cooked all the way through or it may need a little less than an hour depending on your oven. Leave the cake to cool in the tin and then take it out.

note
This is mine and my nan's favourite birthday cake.

Oliver Hudson

I enjoy eating a carvery meal and I like cherries. Sometimes I make my own cakes with no help!

# victoria sandwich

- 100g softened butter ● 100g caster sugar
- 2 standard eggs ● 100g self-raising flour, sifted

Prepare two 18 cm/7" sandwich tins. Cream butter and sugar together until very pale in colour and light and fluffy. Beat in eggs one at a time, adding 1 tbsp flour with each egg. Gently fold in the remaining flour with metal spoon. Transfer to prepared tins and smooth tops with a knife. Bake in the centre of a moderate oven (180°C/350°F/Gas Mark 4) for 25–30 minutes (or until well risen, golden brown and firm). Leave in tins for 2–3 minutes, turn out on wire cooling rack, strip off the paper and leave until cold.

Tianimarier &
Shikira Knight

Tinaimarier: I love pizza, chocolate biscuits and apples. At home daddy cooks good yummy stuff!

Shikira: I love eating... biscuits!

# chocolate fudge cake

- 325g plain chocolate cake covering ● 278g english butter
- 175g caster sugar ● 4 eggs, beaten (size 2)
- 175g self-raising flour ● 50g ground rice
- 10ml (2tsp) vanilla flavouring
- 100g icing sugar, sifted ● 10-15ml (2-3 tsp) coffee essence

Line a 23cm round cake tin with buttered grease-proof paper. Warm half the chocolate cake covering in a bowl over a pan of hot water. Whisk 220g butter and caster sugar together in a bowl until pale and fluffy then gradually beat in eggs, keeping mixture stiff. Lightly beat in the flour with ground rice, vanilla essence and cool but still liquid, chocolate cake covering. Turn the mixture into a cake tin and bake in the oven at 180°C/350°F/Gas Mark 4 for 1¼ hours. Cool in the tin for 30 minutes before turning out. Melt the remaining chocolate cake covering and use to coat the top and side. Whisk the remaining butter in a bowl and beat in the icing sugar and essence. Pipe around cake top using 1cm large star nozzle. Decorate with chocolate toasted almonds.

Lucy McMahon with artwork by Robyn Myatt

I love strawberries and kiwi fruit. I help wash the dishes.

# kate's carrot cake

- 175g carrots ● 2 free range eggs
- 100g soft brown sugar ● 75ml oil
- 100g self-raising flour ● 1 tsp cinnamon
- ½ tsp nutmeg ● 50g desiccated coconut ● 50g raisins

**Topping:**
- 175g cream cheese
- 50g butter ● 100g icing sugar
- few drops vanilla essence

You will need a 7"/18cm lined square tin. Oven temperature 190°C/375°F/Gas Mark 5. Finely grate the carrots. Whisk eggs and sugar together until thick and creamy. Very slowly add oil then add all the other ingredients. Spoon into prepared tin and level the surface. Cook for 20–25 minutes until firm and golden. Cool on wire rack. Mix all topping ingredients together and spoon on top.

Harriet &
William Rogers

Harriet: I like pizza and cherries. I love making cakes.

# yogurt cake

- 125g plain organic yogurt ● 100g caster sugar ● 375g self-raising flour ● 125g organic sunflower oil ● 3 large free-range eggs ● 250g sultanas

Mix yogurt and oil thoroughly, add sugar and eggs and beat well. Add flour and sultanas. Place mixture in a 2lb loaf tin and bake for 1½ hours at 160°C/325°F/Gas Mark 3.

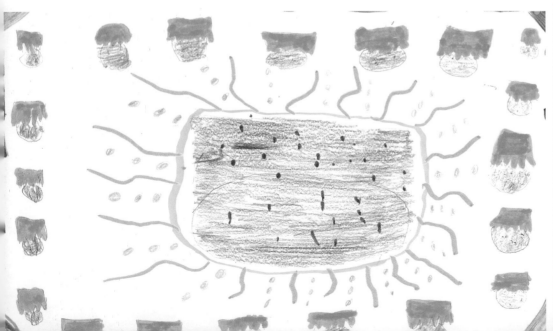

Jack Williams

I like to eat jacket potatoes and brusse sprouts! I sometimes bake cakes.

# lemon curd tarts

- **175g shortcrust pastry**
- **4 tbsp lemon curd**
- **225g curd cheese**
- **2 medium eggs, beaten**
- **50g caster sugar**
- **grated nutmeg**

Roll out the pastry thinly and cut into 9, 4" rounds. Line a 9 hole muffin tin and chill in the fridge for 15 minutes. Put 1 tsp of the lemon curd in the base of each pastry case. Mix together in a separate bowl the curd cheese, eggs and sugar and divide the mixture between the 9 pastry cases. Sprinkle with nutmeg. Bake in oven at 190°C/375°F/ Gas Mark 5 for 20 – 25 minutes until the filling has risen and the pastry is crisp. Dust with icing sugar.

Serves: Makes 9

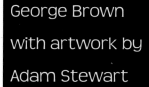

George Brown

with artwork by

Adam Stewart

I love cherries and apples. I help by putting the plates away.

# olivia's chocolate cake

- 100g plain flour, plus extra for dusting ● 150g raspberries
- 4 free-range eggs ● 125g caster sugar ● 30g cocoa powder
- butter for greasing

For the chocolate cream: ● 500ml whipping cream ● 30g cocoa powder ● 30g icing sugar

To decorate: ● chocolate pistoles or buttons ● piped chocolate ● whipped cream

Preheat oven to 180°C. Butter and flour a 25cm cake tin. To make the raspberry puree, blend the raspberries and then press through a sieve to remove any seeds. In a bowl, whisk the eggs and caster sugar together until light and pale. Sift the flour and cocoa powder into a bowl then fold in carefully with a spatula. Pour into the prepared cake tin and bake for 20 – 25 minutes until risen. Remove from the oven and leave in the tin for 10 minutes then turn out onto a wire rack to cool. To make the chocolate cream, pour the whipping cream into a bowl and sift in the cocoa powder and icing sugar and whisk the mixture until thick and creamy. Cut the cake into 3 horizontal layers and place one layer on a serving plate. Spoon half of the raspberry puree over the cake, add a large spoonful of the chocolate cream and spread it all over.

Repeat with a second layer of sponge, puree and cream. Place the remaining layer of sponge on top and press down gently.  Using a palette knife spread the remaining chocolate cream around the sides of the cake and over the top.  Smooth and level the cream with a warm palette knife. To decorate, pipe chocolate cream and whipped cream around the base and top of the cake.  Pipe chocolate over the cream and then arrange chocolate pistoles or buttons on the top.  Personalise the cake with piped chocolate if required.

Olivia Tanner
My favourite food's my chocolate cake! I like apples and grapes as well. At home I chop vegetables and fruit, and mash the potatoes in the 'masher'.

# buns

- 100g butter ● 100g sugar
- 100g self-raising flour ● 3 eggs ● milk ● bun cases

Mix butter and sugar together until creamy.
Carefully mix in the eggs. Fold in the flour and add a
small amount of milk until mixture is smooth. Place
mixture in bun cases and cook at 180°C/Gas Mark 4
for 15 minutes.

Suki & Kayla Elliott
Kayla: I love to eat
pizza and pineapple.
At home I help cook.
Suki: I love lasagne
and strawberries.
I clear away after
eating and I dry the
dishes.

# welsh cakes

- **225g self-raising flour** ● **110g butter**
- **1 egg** ● **handful of sultanas** ● **85g caster sugar**
- **sprinkle mixed spice**

Rub the butter into the flour to make breadcrumbs.
Add the sugar, sultanas, spice and egg. Mix to
combine and form a ball of dough. Roll out the
dough until it is 5mm thick. Cut with a round cutter.
Heat up griddle and place the welsh cake on the
griddle, turn once after 2 minutes. Remove from
griddle when both sides are brown. Dust with sugar
while still warm.

Matthew Farrin

I enjoy eating chicken in
breadcrumbs and cu-
cumber. At home I lay
the table.

# oliver's jam doughnut muffins

● **225g self-raising flour, sifted** ● **2 medium eggs** ● **75g caster sugar** ● **170ml milk** ● **75g butter, melted and cooled slightly** ● **vanilla extract to taste** ● **8 tsp high fruit content jam**
**Topping:** ● **30g golden caster sugar** ● **25g butter, melted** ● **½ tsp ground cinnamon**

Pre-heat oven to 200°C/400°F/Gas Mark 6. Line a muffin tray with 8 cases. In a bowl mix together the milk, butter, eggs, vanilla and sugar. Quickly fold the sifted flour into the wet ingredients. Half fill each case with the mixture then using a teaspoon make a small indentation in each and put in a scant teaspoon of the jam. Cover the jam with the remaining mixture to give a jammy centre. Bake for approximately 25 minutes or until the muffins are well risen and golden brown. Meanwhile mix together the caster sugar and cinnamon for the topping. When the muffins are cooked remove from the oven and place on a wire rack to cool. Whilst still warm brush the tops of the muffins with a little melted butter and roll lightly in the caster sugar and cinnamon mix to give a fine coating.

Oliver Fay

I really like pasta.

# chunky chocolate and banana muffins

- 6 tbsp milk ● 2 eggs ● 150g unsalted butter – melted
- 225g plain flour ● pinch of salt ● 1 tsp baking powder ● 150g golden caster sugar ● 150g plain chocolate, cut into large chunks
- 2 small bananas, mashed

Place 12 paper cases in a deep muffin tin. Preheat the oven to 200°C/400°F/Gas Mark 6. Place the milk, eggs and butter in a bowl and whisk until combined. Sift together the flour, salt and baking powder into a separate bowl. Add the sugar and chocolate to the flour mixture and then stir to combine. Slowly stir in the milk mixture, but do not beat it. Fold in the mashed bananas. Spoon the mixture into the paper cases. Bake for 20 minutes until golden. Cool on a wire rack.

Makes 12 muffins

Alice Howe

My favourite food is chocolate and I like salad as well. At home I cook eggs.

# brownies

- **350g good quality dark chocolate**
- **250g butter** ● **3 large eggs**
- **250g dark muscovado sugar**
- **85g plain flour** ● **1 tsp baking powder**

Preheat oven to 160°C/325°F/Gas Mark 3.  Butter and line base of a shallow cake tin 9" square.  Melt chocolate and butter together, stirring and leave to cool.  Whisk eggs until pale, whisk in sugar until thick and glossy.  Fold in chocolate mix.  Gently fold in sieved flour and baking powder until smooth.  Pour into cake tin and bake for 30-35 minutes.  When cooked it should be soft in the centre but will firm when cooled.  Cook for 1 hour in the tin and then cut into 16 squares and finish cooling on a wired rack.

Nicole Mills

I like eating spaghetti and tomatoes. My mum cooks lots of yummy food!

# apple oatmeal crunch

- **4 or 5 medium cooking apples, cored, peeled and sliced**
- **5 tbsp of dark, soft brown sugar**
- **5 tbsp granulated sugar ● 50g plain flour**
- **75g rolled oats ● 115g melted butter ● 115ml water**
- **225ml whipped or ice cream**

Preheat oven to 190°C/375°F/Gas Mark 5. Spread the sliced apples over the bottom of a greased, shallow baking dish. In a mixing bowl combine the brown sugar, granulated sugar, flour and oats and stir in the melted butter. Spread this mixture over the apples. Pour the water evenly over the top. Bake until the apples are tender – for about 30 minutes. Serve warm or at room temperature with whipped or ice cream.

note
Prepare as above, but mix in ½ teaspoon of ground cinnamon and ¼ teaspoon of ground nutmeg with the sugar, flour and oats.

Sasha Roberts

My favourite food is tuna pasta bake and I like fresh salad. In the kitchen I like baking cakes and fruit crumbles, apple and rhubarb.

# rock buns

- 100g butter - 225g plain flour - 10ml baking powder - 2.5ml ground mixed spice
- grated rind of ½ lemon - 100g demerara sugar - 100g mixed dried fruit
- 1 egg, beaten - 5ml milk

Grease 2 baking sheets. Rub butter into the sifted flour, baking powder and spice until the mixture resembles fine breadcrumbs. Stir in the rind, sugar and fruit. Make a well in the centre and pour in the egg with a little milk if necessary to give a stiff, crumbly consistency. Use 2 forks to shape the mixture into rough heaps on the baking sheets. Bake in the oven at 200°C/400°F/Gas Mark 6 for 15 to 20 minutes.

Serves: Makes 12 buns

Ryan Smith

I like to eat pizza and apples. At home I help by getting my own breakfast.

# matilda cakes

- **1 tbsp syrup** ● **50g sugar** ● **75g margarine**
- **50g chopped cherries** ● **50g sultanas** ● **125g self-raising flour**

Melt margarine, syrup and sugar in a saucepan. Add
remaining ingredients. Mix together and form into
balls. Place on baking tray. Bake for 16-20 minutes
at 190°C/375°F/Gas Mark 4.

Laura Tweedle

I love cheddar cheese
and bananas. At home
I get my sister's
breakfast.

# coconut mice

- **200g tin of condensed milk**
- **250g icing sugar, sifted**
- **175g desiccated coconut**
- **red food dye** ● **sweets for ears**
- **silver cake decorating balls**
- **liquorice bootlaces**

Mix the icing sugar and the condensed milk together in a bowl. Mix in the coconut. Put the mixture into two bowls. Add a few drops of red dye to each bowl and mix it in. Then add a few more drops of dye to one of the bowls. Dip a clean tablespoon into some water and let it drip. Then lift out a big spoonful of the mixture. Pat the spoonful smooth on top. Turn the spoon over and put the shape onto a piece of plastic food wrap. Pinch a nose at the thinner end of the spoon shape. Then add the sweets for ears and silver balls for the eyes. Push a piece of liquorice under the shape as a tail and leave the mouse to harden on a plate. Make more mice – for the baby mice use a teaspoon.

Abigail & Anna Wilson

Abigail: I like roast dinner and apples and carrots. I sometimes do the washing up and set the table.

# crispy bricks

- 1 cup mini marshmallows ● 2 cups puffed rice cereal ● 2 tbsp sugar ● 1 tbsp cocoa
- 2 tsp water ● 2 tbsp butter or margarine
- ice-cube trays

Ask a grown-up helper to melt 1 tbsp butter over a low heat and add the marshmallows. Add the puffed rice and stir together. Use a teaspoon to pack the mixture into the ice-cube trays. Leave to cool then put them in the fridge to set hard. To make icing, mix the remaining butter and sugar until you have a creamy mixture. Add cocoa powder and water to make a smooth paste. When bricks have set remove them from ice-cube trays. Use the chocolate icing mixture as cement to stick the bricks together.

Phoebe Richardson

I love to eat chinese food and strawberries. At home I lay the table.

# melting moments

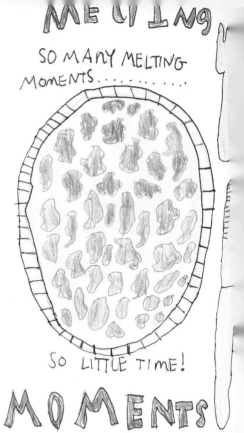

- **100g butter** ● **75g caster sugar** ● **1 egg yolk, beaten** ● **few drops vanilla essence**
- **150g self raising flour** ● **50g crushed cornflakes**

Grease two baking sheets. Cream the butter and sugar together until pale and fluffy. Add in the beaten egg yolk. Add the vanilla flavouring and stir in the flour to give a smooth dough and divide into about 24 portions. Form each piece into a ball and roll in the crushed cornflakes. Place the balls on the baking sheet and bake in the oven at 190°C/375°F/Gas Mark 5 for 12–20 minutes. Cool on the baking sheets for a few moments before lifting out onto a wire rack.

note
These crisp, crunch biscuits melt in the mouth – hence their name. A freshly baked batch will soon disappear!! Variation – instead of cornflakes use oats. Press half a glace cherry in the centre of each biscuit.

Daniel Jones

Favourite food...chips
I like pineapple as well
In the kitchen I help
my mum cook meals
for our family.

# tom's chocolate hedgehogs

**● 75g plain chocolate ● 1.5 tbsp golden syrup ● 5g black & 5g white ready made royal icing ● 10 matchmakers chocolate orange flavour**

Melt chocolate in a bowl over a pan of boiling water. Using oven gloves lift the bowl out of the pan and leave to cool for a few minutes. Stir in the golden syrup until the mixture forms a thick paste. Wrap in cling film. Place chocolate in the fridge for one hour. Take out of the fridge and leave to soften. Cut into equal sections. Roll each section into rounds and then form the hedgehog face. The royal icing can used to make eyes. Now add the spines to your hedgehogs using small pieces of matchmakers. Place in fridge for 10 minutes. Eat straight from fridge.

Thomas Coles

I love mashed potatoes and peas in the pod. Sometimes I help to make omelettes.

# shortbread

- **175g plain flour, sifted** ● **pinch of salt**
- **100g butter** ● **50g caster sugar**
- **grated rind of 1 lemon** ● **icing sugar to dust**

Grease and flour a baking tray. Put the flour and salt in a mixing bowl. Rub in the butter then stir in the sugar and lemon rind. Lightly work the mixture together until it forms a small stiff ball of dough. Roll into a 20cm/8" circle and place on the baking tray. Pinch the edges, prick the middle all over with a fork and cut the shortbread into 8 wedges. Chill for 15 minutes. Bake in a moderate oven (160°C/325F°/Gas Mark 3) for 40 minutes or until pale golden. Leave on the baking tray for a few minutes then cool completely on a wire rack.

Josiah Caunter

My favourite food is pizza and chips. I like to eat apples as well. dad normally cooks but mum cooks when he's at work.

# chocolate fork biscuits

- 100g soft margarine
- 50g caster sugar
- 120g self raising flour
- 15g cocoa powder

Preheat oven to 180°C/350°F/Gas Mark 4. Lightly grease 2 baking trays. Put the margarine into a bowl and soften with a wooden spoon. Gradually beat in the sugar and mix in the flour and cocoa. Bring the mixture together with your hands to form a dough, divide the dough into balls about the size of a walnut and place well apart on the prepared baking trays. Dip a fork in a little water and use this to flatten the biscuits. Bake in the oven for about 15-20 minutes until browned. Lift off the baking tray and leave to cool completely on a wire rack.

Alice Hayward

I love pancakes and avocado salad. In the kitchen I cook pancakes and have them with lots of lemon and sugar!

# munchy flapjacks

- 175g butter ● 125g soft light-brown sugar
- 55g golden syrup ● 350g porridge oats

Turn the oven to 180°C/350°F/Gas Mark 4. Place the butter, sugar and syrup in a saucepan over a low heat for 2-3 minutes, stirring until melted. Remove from the heat and mix in the porridge oats. Pour the mixture into a lined and greased baking try. Press down well. Bake in the oven for 25-30 minutes. Remove from oven and leave to cool for 10 minutes. Cut into squares and allow to cool completely in the tin. Carefully remove the flapjacks from the tin using a knife.

Meg Musgrave

My favourite meal is roast lamb with carrots. I help my mum by getting the knives and forks out.

# mini cookies

- 125g butter ● 125g golden caster sugar
- 1 large egg, beaten ● 1 ripe banana, mashed
- 175g self-raising flour ● 1 tsp mixed spice
- 2 tbsp milk ● 100g chopped mixed nuts
- 55g raisins

Pre-heat oven to 190°C/375°F/Gas Mark 5. Cream together the butter and sugar. Gradually add the egg to the mixture beating well each time. Mash the banana and add, beating until the mixture is smooth. Sieve in the flour and spice. Fold in using a spatula. Add the milk to give a soft consistency. Fold in the nuts and fruit. Drop dessert spoons of the mixture onto greased baking trays. Space cookies well apart about 9 on each tray. Bake in the oven for 15–20 minutes. Take out of the oven and leave for 5 minutes before moving to a cooling rack.

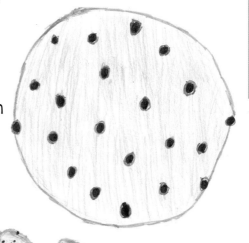

Luke Musgrave

My favourite meal is roast lamb! I like bananas as well. I enjoy making cakes.

# simple chocolate shortbread

● **125g softened butter** ● **50g caster sugar**
● **3 tbsp milk** ● **160g plain flour** ● **15g cocoa powder**

Preheat the oven to 350°F/180°C/Gas Mark 4. Sieve the

flour and cocoa into a mixing bowl, stir in the sugar.

Cut up the butter and add to the dry ingredients, rub

in with your fingers until the mixture resembles fine

breadcrumbs. Add a tablespoon of milk, mix everything

together with your hands to form a ball of dough. Roll out

the dough with a rolling pin and create your own shapes.

Put the shortbread in the top half of the oven for 15-20

minutes then put them on a wire rack to cool.

Simple Chocolate

Short bread

Abbie Campbell

My favourite foods
are mussels and fruit
salad. In the kitchen I
bake chocolate cakes
and decorate them
with more chocolate!

# rice krispie cakes

● **300g rice krispies** ● **50g butter** ● **6 mars bars**

Melt the butter in a saucepan then add the chopped
up mars bars. Stir continuously over a low heat
until they have melted then add the rice krispies.
Mix everything together and spoon into paper cake
cases. Put them in the fridge for 10 minutes.

Tom Pierce

My favourite food is
pasta bake. I like to eat
apples as well. At home
I help with the washing
up.

# yummy chocolate biscuits

- 100g butter or margarine ● 50g caster sugar
- 40g self raising flour ● 25g drinking chocolate or sieved cocoa powder ● few drops vanilla essence
- For the icing: ● 50g butter ● 100g icing sugar, sieved

Cream together the butter and sugar until pale and fluffy. Stir in the flour and drinking chocolate or cocoa powder, add vanilla essence to taste. Roll the mixture into 24 balls the size of a marble and place on a baking tray. Flatten with a fork dipped in cold water. Bake for 10 minutes and allow to cool. Beat icing sugar into butter. Sandwich together with icing and dust with icing sugar.

Abbie Tweedle

I love chinese food and I like cucumber. At home I help with the washing up.

# celebrity chefs & talented teachers

# maple baked pork fillet with black pudding and pear

- 1 x 150g pork fillet ● 50g black pudding ● 3 tbsp maple syrup
- 1 pear ● 50ml red wine ● 100ml beef stock ● 1 knob butter
- 1 chopped shallot

Roast pork in sauté pan for 2-3 minutes, bake in oven at 200°C for further 10-12 minutes and half way through baking coat the pork with the maple syrup. After cooking, leave pork to rest on a wire rack for 2 minutes. Slice black pudding, drizzle with olive oil and cook for 3 minutes in oven at 200°C. Slice pear, coat in olive oil and char-grill on both sides for 2 minutes. For the sauce, sauté shallot for 1 minute then add the wine. Reduce the wine by half, add the stock and reduce liquid by two thirds. Strain and whisk in a knob of butter. To serve, slice pork and arrange alternately with slices of black pudding over the char-grilled pear and drizzle red wine sauce around it.

James & Chris Tanner

# mich's marvellous mountain of mash

- **1kg floury potatoes such as maris piper** ● **2 tbsp olive oil** ● **25g butter** ● **1 large onion, finely chopped** ● **250g sliced mushrooms** ● **2tbsp chopped parsley** ● **100g fresh peas** ● **100g grated cheddar cheese** ● **salt and pepper**

Scrub the potatoes and cut into large chunks. Place them in a large saucepan, cover with lightly salted water and bring to the boil. Reduce the heat and cook for 15 minutes. Meanwhile, heat the olive oil in a large saucepan and sauté the onion gently for 5 minutes until translucent and soft. Add the mushrooms, peas, and 2 tbsp water and cook, covered for a further 5 minutes until the mushrooms have softened. Drain the potatoes and return to the pan. Place the lid on and wearing oven gloves give the pan a hefty shake to break up the potatoes. Season the potatoes with freshly ground black pepper (no need to add more salt) and add the butter. Remove the mushrooms from the heat and transfer them into the potatoes. Add the fresh parsley and stir together. Transfer to a large ovenproof baking dish and sprinkle the grated cheese on top. Bake in a preheated oven – 180°C for 25 minutes until golden brown.

Mich Turner

Serves: 4

# ainsley harriott's seared chicken with mango salsa and sweet potato wedges

- 900g even-sized sweet potatoes (orange fleshed if possible)
- 3 tbsp light olive oil ● 4 chicken fillets, each about 150g each
- knob of unsalted butter

For the salsa: ● 1 ripe firm mango ● 1 small red onion, finely chopped ● 1 red chilli, seeded and finely chopped ● 2 heaped tbsp chopped fresh herbs (flat leaf parsley, coriander and chives) ● juice of 1 lime ● sea salt and freshly ground black pepper

Preheat the oven to 200°C/400°F/Gas 6. Wash the sweet potatoes and cut them into wedges. Place two tablespoons of the olive oil in a roasting tin with a teaspoon of the salt. Add the wedges and toss until they are all well coated in the oil. Bake for 35-40 minutes, turning once until completely tender and lightly golden.  Meanwhile, make the mango salsa. Peel the mango and cut the flesh into 1cm/ ½ in dice. Place in a bowl with the red onion, chilli, herbs and lime juice. Season to taste and set aside at room temperature to allow the flavours to combine.  Heat a large heavy based frying pan over a fairly high heat. Season the chicken fillets generously. Add the remaining tablespoon of olive oil and the butter.

When the butter is foaming, add the chicken fillets skin-side down and cook for 6 minutes, making sure they don't brown too much. Turn the chicken fillets over and cook for another 2-4 minutes until just tender, then remove the pan from the heat and leave the chicken to rest in a warm place for 5 to 10 minutes. To serve, place a pile of the sweet potato wedges on the bottom of each serving plate. Cut the chicken fillets into slices on the diagonal and gently fan out, then arrange on top of the wedges, add a good spoonful of salsa to the side and drizzle the remainder around the edges of each plate.

Serves: 4

Ainsley Harriott

Just because you are trying to keep to a healthy diet doesn't mean that food can't taste and look delicious.

# smoked haddock, salmon and prawn pie with a spinach topping

- 500g floury potatoes, such as maris piper, cut into chunks
- 500g frozen spinach, thawed and thoroughly drained
- 700ml skimmed milk ● grated fresh nutmeg ● ground black pepper
- 2 fresh bay leaves ● I whole clove ● 250g salmon fillet (in one piece)
- 250g haddock fillet (in one piece) ● 25g unsalted butter
- I onion, finely diced ● 25g cornflour ● I tsp anchovy essence
- 2 tbsp chopped parsley ● 1/2 tsp soft thyme leaves
- I tsp dry english mustard powder ● 200g large peeled prawns (raw or cooked) ● 50g gruyère, grated ● 25g freshly grated parmesan
- sugar snap peas ● roasted cherry tomatoes

Preheat the oven to 200°C/400°F/Gas Mark 6.  To make the topping, steam the potatoes for 15-20 minutes or until completely tender. Drain and return to the pan with the thawed spinach over a gentle heat for a couple of minutes to dry out, shaking the pan occasionally to prevent the potatoes sticking to the bottom. Mash the potatoes then beat in up to 100ml milk and season to taste with nutmeg and pepper.  Place 600ml milk in a sauté pan with the bay leaves, clove and a pinch of nutmeg. Add the salmon and haddock fillets and poach for 6-8 minutes or until the fish is just tender.

Transfer the fish fillets to a plate with a fish slice and set aside until they are cool enough to handle, then flake the flesh, discarding the skin and any bones. Set aside. Strain the poaching liquid and set aside.  Melt the butter in a large non-stick pan. Add the onion and cook for 6-8 minutes until the onion has softened but not coloured, stirring occasionally. Pour in the reserved poaching milk. Mix the cornflour to a paste with a little of the remaining milk then add a little warm milk from the pan and return to the rest of the liquid, stirring all the time. Reduce the heat and simmer gently for 10 minutes, stirring occasionally until slightly reduced and thickened.  Stir the anchovy essence, parsley, thyme and mustard powder into the sauce. Fold in the reserved flaked fish and prawns, then season to taste. Spoon the fish mixture into an ovenproof dish, that is at least 2.25 litres in size. Allow a light skin to form, then carefully spread over the spinach and potato mash to cover. Smooth over with a palette knife and fluff up with a fork. Mix together the gruyère and parmesan and sprinkle over the top, then bake for 20-25 minutes or until the cheese is bubbling and golden.  Serve at once with the vegetables.

Serves: 6

Anthony Worrall Thompson

A fish pie is one of the most comforting meals and this version is no exception. I make this when I need a really filling meal.

# wells-next-the-sea crab spring rolls

● **500g crab meat** ● **I handful chopped coriander** ● **2 tablespoons mayonnaise** ● **¼ red chilli** ● **¼ green chilli** ● **I lemon juice and zest** ● **I lime juice and zest** ● **salt & pepper to taste** ● **sweet chilli sauce** ● **3 tbsp fish sauce** ● **2 spring roll wrappers per spring roll** ● **I egg for egg wash**

Mix all of the above other than the wrappers and egg wash together and check for taste. Lay out wrappers and place a line of mixture down the middle of one. Roll up like a large cigar. Paint end of wrapper with egg wash to stick it down. Repeat rolling process with second wrapper. Deep fry at 180°C for 2 minutes. Slice and serve with sweet chilli dipping sauce.

Serves: Makes 10

Chris Coubrough

# chana chaat chickpea curry

- **2 tbsp vegetable oil ● 1 tsp finely chopped garlic**
- **2-3 tsp mild curry powder ● 3 tbsp finely chopped onion ● 1 tbsp tomato puree ● 400g canned chick peas ● 1 fresh tomato chopped ● chopped green chilli to taste (optional) ● fresh coriander to taste ● salt to taste**

Heat the oil. Stir-fry the garlic for 30 seconds, then add the curry powder and stir-fry for a while more. Add all the remaining ingredients, and stir-fry for about 2 minutes. Remove from the heat and serve hot, or allow to cool. For the cold version serve the chana on a bed of salad or mix the two together.

Serves: 4

Pat Chapman

The three minute curry. That's all it takes to make it. Fast, simple, nutritious, filling and tasty! You can even serve it on toast.

# carbonnade of beef with double potato topping

- 3 tablespoons sunflower oil ● 900g diced braising steak
- 1 large red onion, sliced into chunky wedges
- 2 cloves garlic, crushed ● 225g chestnut mushrooms, halved, or quartered if large ● 40g flour ● 300ml lager
- 150ml beef stock ● 1 tablespoon tomato puree
- 1 tablespoon light brown sugar ● 175g sundried tomatoes, snipped into four

Topping: ● 450g sweet potatoes ● 450g old potatoes

Pre-heat oven to 200°C/400°F/Gas Mark 6. You will need a deep ovenproof dish about 3 pint capacity (not too wide). Heat two tablespoons of oil in large non-stick frying pan or casserole dish. Brown the meat over a high heat until browned all over (you may need to do this in batches), remove meat from pan with a slotted spoon and set aside. Add remaining tablespoon of oil to same unwashed pan, add onion, garlic and mushrooms and fry over high heat for a few mins. Return meat to the pan, sprinkle in the flour, gradually blend in the lager and blend in stock, mixing continuously over a high heat until smooth. Bring to the boil, add sugar, tomato puree, sundried tomatoes and salt and pepper.

Cover, reduce heat and cook so just simmering for about 1½ hours or until meat is tender. Taste for seasoning and set aside to get completely cold. For the topping, peel both lots of potatoes and cut into even sized chunks. Cook in boiling salted water until tender, drain and mash with salt and pepper to taste. Once the casserole is cold, tip into an ovenproof serving dish and top with the potato topping. Heat in pre-heated oven for about 30-40 mins until piping hot.

This recipe is perfect for a cold winter's day to serve with winter veg. The mushrooms want to be quite chunky – if they are small leave them whole. Any type of lager will do – a bottle of becks is about ½ a pint! This dish freezes well (without the potato topping).

Serves: 6

Lucy Young

Recipe taken from secrets from a country kitchen (ebury press) by lucy young

# chardonnay chicken with artichoke hearts

- 1 tbsp olive oil ● 15g butter ● 8 chicken thighs on the bone without skin, seasoned ● 2 large onions, roughly chopped ● 2 cloves garlic, crushed ● 1 tsp sugar
- 25g flour ● 300ml chardonnay or dry white wine
- 200g small chestnut mushrooms, whole
- 400g can artichoke hearts, drained, cut in half
- 2 tbsp full fat crème fraiche
- 4 tbsp chopped parley

Take a large deep frying pan, add butter and oil. Brown the thighs all over and lift out. Add onions, garlic and sugar to the remaining oil in the pan over a high heat and fry for a couple of minutes. Turn the heat down, cover and soften the onion for about 15 mins. Remove lid, return to high heat and brown onion.

Sprinkle in the flour. Add wine and stir well. Bring to the boil until thickened and blended. Return chicken to the pan with the mushrooms, season, bring to the boil for a few mins. Cover, lower the heat and simmer for about 35–45 mins until chicken is tender. Add artichokes and crème fraiche, check seasoning and stir in half the parsley. Sprinkle with remaining parsley and serve.

Serves: 6-8

Mary Berry
Recipe from Cook Now
Eat Later by Mary Berry

This special chicken casserole goes really well with creamy mashed potato.

# meatballs with tomato fondue, to serve with spaghetti

- 900g freshly minced beef ● 150g onion, finely chopped
- 1 clove of garlic, crushed ● 2 tbsp freshly chopped herbs, like marjoram or  rosemary ● salt and freshly ground pepper
- 2 tbsp olive oil ● 1 egg, beaten  ● 3 tbsp olive oil ● 110g onion, sliced
- 1 garlic clove, crushed ● salt, sugar and freshly ground pepper
- 2 x 400g tins of tomatoes. ● 150g grated mozzarella
- 450g pasta , such as spaghetti

Heat 2 tbsp of olive oil in a heavy stainless steel saucepan over a gentle heat and add the onion and garlic. Cover and sweat for 4 minutes, until soft and a little golden, allow to cool.  In a bowl, mix the minced beef with the cold sweated onion and garlic. Add the herbs, and the beaten egg. Season the mixture with salt and pepper.

Fry off a tiny bit to check the seasoning and adjust if necessary. Divide the mixture into about 24 round balls. Cover the meatballs and refrigerate until required.  Meanwhile, make the tomato fondue.  Heat the oil in a stainless steel saucepan. Add the sliced onion and the crushed garlic, toss until coated, cover and sweat on a gentle heat until soft and even a tiny bit golden.

Slice the tinned tomatoes and add with all the juice to the onion mixture. Season the contents with salt, freshly ground pepper and sugar. Cook the tomatoes uncovered for approximately 30 minutes or until the tomato softens. While this is cooking make the meatballs. Heat up a frying pan and cook the meatballs, for about 10 minutes, in about 3 tbsp olive oil. Meanwhile cook the pasta in a large pot of boiling salted water. When the meatballs are cooked, place them in a grill-proof dish with the tomato fondue and the cooked, drained pasta. Toss together, sprinkle with the grated mozzarella, and put under a grill to let the cheese melt. Serve straight away.

Serves: 6-8

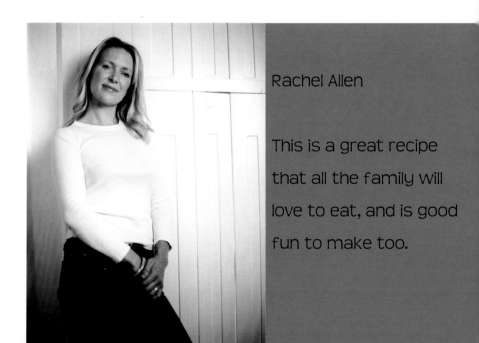

Rachel Allen

This is a great recipe that all the family will love to eat, and is good fun to make too.

# vegetable fritters

- **2 large peeled potatoes** ● **1 courgette**
- **1 small carrot** ● **1 egg**

Grate all the vegetables by hand or in a processor. Put in a sieve with a saucer on top and squeeze out any liquid. Beat the egg and mix in a bowl with vegetables. Add seasoning or nutmeg if liked. Heat some oil in a frying pan, spoon some mixture in and flatten. Fry well until crispy on both sides. For a homemade tomato sauce to go with it, fry an onion and add some tinned tomatoes and tomato puree and blend once cooked.

carrot

cucumber

Fran McLoughlin

Teacher

This is a family favou

and different vegeta

can be substituted.

It goes well with a

homemade tomato

sauce, garlic bread ar

salad.

# stuffed peppers

- **4 large peppers** ● **450g mince**
- **1 chopped onion** ● **1 tin chopped tomatoes**
- **2 tbsp rice** ● **tomato puree**
- **1 tsp cinnamon** ● **1 tsp nutmeg** ● **1 tsp dried parsley** ● **1 tsp dried mint**

Cut round stalks of peppers and remove (keep them for later in the recipe), de-seed and rinse out peppers. Fry mince in a little oil until browned, add onion, tomato puree, herbs, spices and tinned tomatoes, stir and allow to simmer for 20 mins. Add the uncooked rice and stir. Allow mixture to cool and then stuff the mixture tightly into the peppers, replacing the stalks as plugs. Pour any remaining mixture over the top. Place peppers into large, lidded casserole dish in the oven at 180°C for about 1 hour or until the peppers and rice look ready.

Serves: 4

Su Herbert
Teaching Assistant

Artwork by Kyle Whitford-Robson

# quick fruit cake

- **2 mugs self raising flour** ● **1 mug mixed fruit**
- **1 mug brown sugar** ● **1 mug milk**
- **1-2 tsp mixed spice**

Put all ingredients in a mixing bowl and mix well,

then pour into a greased and lined 1lb loaf tin. Cook

for approximately 1 hour at 180°C/Gas Mark 4-5.

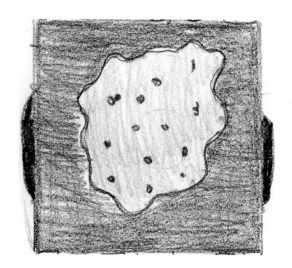

Vicky Bingham
Teaching Assistant
Artwork by Ben
Vinecombe & Emma
Williams
Ben: I love to eat
chocolate and
apples. I help with
the washing up.

# yealmpton school pasta bake

- **350g of your favourite pasta** ● **olive oil**
- **1 large onion** ● **2 tins chopped tomatoes** ● **1 tbsp tomato puree**
- **1 tsp mixed herbs** ● **1 large pepper, chopped**
- **2 cloves of crushed garlic**
- **salt & pepper** ● **cheddar cheese, grated**

Cook pasta until almost cooked (al dente). Fry off onions in a pan with a little olive oil. Add mixed herbs, garlic and pepper. Cook until onions are soft.

Add tomatoes and tomato puree. Bring to the boil and simmer for 20 mins. Mix cooked pasta into the sauce and place in an oven-proof dish, sprinkling with grated cheese.

Bake in oven at Gas Mark 5/190°C for 15-20 mins.

note
For a smoother sauce you can liquidise it before adding to the pasta. Add other ingredients for variety e.g. courgettes, carrots, bacon, mushrooms, etc.

Chris Collum
School chef

# thanks!

A huge thank you to everyone who has been involved along the way in producing Kids on Toast; the children (and parents) for providing their delicious recipes and great artwork; the teachers of Yealmpton Primary School and especially Alison Harrop for all the support and in-school fundraising that helped us reached our target; the celebrity chefs who kindly donated recipes for the book. Thanks also to the Marine Biological Association (MBA) for the use of their facilities for the design work, in particular Guy Baker and Fiona Crouch for their help; thanks to James Wolfe School who started it all in Greenwich and allowed us to use their marvellous design.

But most of all thanks must go to the hardworking cookbook team of parent volunteers who coordinated, fundraised, photographed, collected recipes and pictures, typed, edited, and then put together the final book: Cathie Beaumont, Ally Green, Basia Howard-Harwood, Lindsay Lloyd, Tess Monk, Helen Parr, Judith Snawdon, Steph Tanner and Deb Wiseman.

Well done to Sycamore Class who won the cover competition, and to Alex Milham for winning the title competition.